MW00884647

How I Found Buddha on the Trading Floor

By

Rob Kovell

For my dad.

Contents

Part I

Becoming a Trader

I was ten years old when my mother was diagnosed with breast cancer. Fourteen when my father had his foot amputated. Seventeen when Dad started requiring dialysis twice a week to keep his kidneys functioning. By the time I was eighteen, my father was going blind, could barely walk and, after fighting it for as long as possible, he finally quit his last and favorite outdoor activity: a round of golf played at the same public course every Sunday with the same two friends. He had been an athlete all his life -- skiing, hiking, water-skiing, boating, golf, tennis; he loved them all. Then, in his late fifties with his health failing, his world diminished for he could no longer do any of them.

When I was nineteen, I remember coming home from college and finding Dad sitting alone in the dark living room wearing pressed slacks, a wool cardigan on top of a white dress shirt, wingtip shoes, and he had his hand balanced on his cane as if he were ready to go somewhere. He hadn't been well enough to work for a few years and because he was stockbroker who earned only commissions, he was quickly accumulating debt to pay the medical bills that kept arriving every week. Sitting in the dark that afternoon, my father looked like a man convicted and sentenced to life but dressed in his finest clothes to report to prison. The debt, which he knew would be left to my mother, was killing him faster than any of his medical maladies. Standing there undetected, witnessing Dad's undisguised pain and sadness, I knew I had to do something. There was, of course, no way for me to improve his health but I could do something to ease his financial worry. I needed to make money fast. I knew my dream of studying literature and becoming a writer wasn't going to get me there. I needed a different career path.

Even though my dad was a stockbroker for most of my life, I knew almost nothing about the market and very little about it interested me beyond the enthralling scenes in movies like *Trading Places* and *Quicksilver*, and on the evening news. The intensity, the pureness of greed, and the ordered chaos –it was palpable through the TV screen and I loved it.

During Christmas break in my third year of college, Dad and I were watching the evening news together when a scene from one of the exchanges aired during the nightly business report. I asked if he knew anyone who could help me find a summer internship on a trading floor. He said he would make some calls to see if anything was available but made no comment on my sudden career shift.

At dinner a few nights later, he told me he had called around but that summer internships were popular and almost impossible to get. My mom asked what we were talking about and I told her that I wanted to work on a trading floor.

"My godson, Bill Grebitus, works on a trading floor in San Francisco," she said, without hesitation. "We should talk to him."

I had been prepared to move to Chicago or New York for the summer, so I was thrilled to discover there was a trading floor an hour away from my parents' home, only a half an hour from my college campus. Though our families were close, I barely knew my mother's godson. He was grown up and living on his own before I was old enough to remember him firsthand. Still, Bill Grebitus was already a part of our family lore. When I was very young we took a trip with the Grebitus family to Occidental Beach in Northern California. I was swimming in the breakers when I got pulled away from shore by the current and was struggling to make it back to safety.

"Bill Grebitus saved your life," became the start of a favorite story told countless times by my parents.

The next night, I called Bill at his home in Orinda, California, and told him how fascinated I was with trading floors and how I hoped to find a summer job on one. After a short discussion, he offered me a job as a runner for his firm on the options trading floor of the Pacific Stock Exchange.

I accepted calmly and carefully took down the number of his floor manager whom I was to call for further instructions. After thanking Bill profusely, I placed the phone receiver back in its cradle and let loose a cry of joy so loud the neighbors called to make sure everything was all right.

Bill Grebitus had rescued me again.

I worked on that trading floor for the next seventeen years and continued trading options for the next twenty-five. My career was wildly rewarding: I built my own firm with fifty employees operating in San Francisco and Chicago. We became the largest trading group on the Pacific, and I became the largest trader.

In the mid-1990s, my post accounted for nearly a quarter of the entire trading floor's volume. In July of 2000, I sold most of my floor trading business to Knight Financial (NITE) for an undisclosed but life changing sum. A year after the sale, I left the floor to take a two-year sabbatical, returning to trading when I was recruited by a Chicago market making firm called PEAK6 to start their San Francisco trading desk. They had never had a presence outside of Chicago before but over the next seven years I built a desk comprised of fifteen traders managing one hundred million dollars, before retiring from finance in my late forties. The financial rewards of trading were larger than I had dreamed and I have enjoyed the money that I earned; but the biggest reward I got from trading was Buddha's wisdom. With this wisdom I developed an inner stillness that still allows me to think clearly and calmly in the most volatile situations.

When we think of Buddhists, many of us have an image of a skinny Asian man in orange monk's robes, or of hippies living on a commune growing and eating their own organic vegetables, or of the eastern ascetic monks malnourished and begging for alms. Almost nobody associates the materialism and greed that are on vivid display on trading floors with the spirituality and peace of the Buddha. It is important to note the Buddha himself rejected the rigor of self-denial as rigorously as he had previously rejected its opposite, the life of opulence and wealth.

In ancient Buddhist texts, the Buddha's *creation story* usually goes something like this: the Buddha was an actual man, born Siddhartha Gautama, in Lumbini (present day Nepal) around 500 b.c.e. Siddhartha Gautama was born a prince into a wealthy and powerful ruling family, and was heir to his father's kingdom. Soon after his birth, his father, King Suddhudona, hired the most famous and revered oracle of the time to tell his newborn son's fortune. The seer told the king that his son would surely be great but he would *either* be a great heir to the throne, ruler of people *or,* if he came to know suffering, a great spiritual leader.

Suddhodona's greatest desire was for his son, Siddhartha, to take over his rule and build on the family's legacy, so the *or* in the seer's vision caused him great anxiety. He asked the seer how he could guarantee his son would be a ruler.

"Prevent your son from seeing the suffering of mankind and he will stay and lead your people to greatness," the seer told the king.

Determined to preserve his legacy and kingdom by having his son inherit the throne, the king surrounded Siddhartha with everything a boy could desire inside their castle grounds. What's more, the king took great pains to shield his son from seeing anyone sick, suffering, or old, so whenever young Siddhartha left the palace grounds, his father sent servants ahead to clear the path of any signs of it. According to Buddhist legend, this went on for many years. When Siddhartha reached the age of twenty-nine, he was already skeptical about the world his father allowed him to see and was very curious what the world would look like if he weren't a prince. He decided that he had to escape his father's vigilance and see the world for himself. He enlisted his lifelong servant, Channa, to help disguise him as a servant so he could escape the palace undetected.

The day Siddhartha and Channa left the palace is called The Day of Four Sights.

Soon after they passed through the palace gates, an old man, stooped and frail, approached their chariot to beg for assistance. Siddhartha was shocked by the sight of the old man and asked Channa what was wrong with him. Channa explained that the man was old and destitute. He told Siddhartha the man had once been young like them but grew old, as all men do. For the first time in his life, Siddhartha realized his body would fail him as he grew old. This was the *First Sight*.

Continuing down the road, the two young men encountered the *Second Sight*: a sick man lying on the side of the road in obvious misery. Siddhartha, deeply saddened by the man's suffering, asked Channa what was causing it. Channa explained that the man was sick, that all men get sick and that Siddhartha, too, might someday battle an illness.

As the two men made their way back to the palace, they came upon a funeral procession made up of grieving relatives carrying a dead body aloft on a stretcher. Again, Siddhartha asked Channa about it and was told that they, too, would someday die. This was the *Third Sight*.

Profoundly shaken by all he had seen and learned, Siddhartha told Channa to hurry back to the palace. But as they raced back, Siddhartha noticed an ascetic monk sat cross-legged meditating by the side of the road. Under a shady tree, simply clothed and empty-handed except for an alms bowl, the monk was surrounded by the suffering of the world and yet he wore a serene smile that radiated peace. The prince told Channa to stop and asked him about the monk. Channa explained that the man was a *Samana*, a monk who had renounced the world and its material pleasures to seek the true meaning of life through meditation and prayer. Samanas wander the world in poverty, Channa told his master, wearing only plain robes and carrying only one possession: a single bowl for alms. Once a day, the monks traded their wisdom for the only food they allowed themselves. Siddhartha was captivated by the serene Samana and knew immediately he would abandon his wealth, his power and all he had ever known to become one. He returned to his father's palace that night, kissed his wife and young son goodbye, and, with Channa's assistance, fled into the night riding his favorite white horse.

Channa and Siddhartha rode swiftly away from the palace until they reached the Anoma River, where Siddhartha dismounted. He carefully removed his jewelry and royal clothing and gave them to his loyal servant to return to his father. Then he picked up his sword for the final time and cut off his beautiful long hair. After handing the sword to Channa, he put on a simple monk's robe and bid farewell to his friend. Channa protested, begging the prince to allow him to come along, but the prince would not be swayed. Channa wept as he watched Siddhartha Gautama walk alone into the night no longer a Prince.

Although the details vary in different accounts, these are the basics, the bedrock of the Buddha's creation story. It seems to be more of a literary expression of events than a literal history, but we do know that many of the facts are true.

History confirms that Prince Siddhartha Gautama was indeed born into a powerful family sometime around 500 b.c.e. Scholars have also confirmed that he lived in his father's palace until he was twenty-nine years old. And whether or not he had been shocked into his departure by seeing suffering for the first time or whether it was just the original "mid-life crisis," we know that Siddhartha *did* leave his wealthy family to become a wandering ascetic monk.

For six years Siddhartha walked around India in the Samana tradition, spending his time studying, meditating and teaching. He ate a single meal a day and slept outside with only his robe to protect him, embracing self-denial as fervidly as the most austere monks. For the first few years of his life as a Samana, Siddhartha followed various teachers, but ultimately, he was a teacher himself and had five followers.

And yet even after years of practice, Siddhartha did not feel any closer to peace. He tried intensifying his austerity, trading in his cotton garb for a robe of the coarsest material, which irritated his skin. He tried restricting his food intake to a single nut or leaf per day. Still, he struggled to find inner peace. Near starvation, he finally succumbed to exhaustion and collapsed in a river. As legend has it, Siddhartha was close to drowning when a young village girl saw him and helped him to a nearby tree where she gave him food and water and comforted him. Siddhartha regained his strength quickly and, sitting there under the tree, he recalled a similar tree he had sat under as a boy.

Young Siddhartha had gone out into the fields with his father and his father's men to watch how they managed the crops. It was a long, hot, and mostly uneventful day and the boy grew bored. He sat down under a rose apple tree and let his mind wander to pass the time. With nothing to see in the fields, young Siddhartha began attending to his breath, mindfully breathing deeply and slowly. All these many years later, near starvation and under a different tree, he recalled that the focused breathing had dispelled his anxious feelings and made him more acutely aware of the beauty of his surroundings. So, an older and wearier Siddhartha once again focused on his breathing, taking deep slow breaths until he achieved the same heightened awareness and clarity had felt as a boy. His mind began to fill with wonder and gratitude and the sadness he had been feeling dissipated.

With this newly found peace, Siddhartha realized austerity was as harmful as its opposite and he rejected asceticism, just as he had previously rejected opulence. He sought a middle way. A life without luxury, but also without need. He began to teach the *Four Noble Truths* and the *Eightfold Noble Path* as the wisest, kindest ways to increase awareness of and appreciation for the surrounding world.

Siddhartha's noble path was the middle way and is indeed the way to find peace.

Though created by an ancient monk a few thousand years ago, the Eightfold Noble Path does not preclude competing in the modern workplace to provide for yourself and your family; in fact, it facilitates it. As a trader, I worked hard to earn enough money to take care of my family and myself, but the middle way also meant taking time away from work in order to *take care of my family and myself.* The problem is that time is money in trading. If you are off the floor when the best trade of the day, month or year comes in, you miss it. A trader's biggest fear. So, most traders never miss a minute at their post when the market is open, afraid to leave a single dollar on the table that they could instead take home. I learned that my own long-term results, and those of the many traders I managed, actually improved when we took regular breaks from the intensity of trading, even if that meant missing a good trade or two.

In print and on film, Apple creator Steve Jobs has been portrayed as displaying a lack of kindness, an indifference toward his family and an inability to be emotionally intimate with others. Yet he remains a global idol. Almost anybody you ask would trade lives with Jobs in a flash.

Not me.

I wouldn't want the money nor would the achievements matter if I could not love those around me and, and in turn, be loved by them. Inventing the iPod and the iPhone would mean nothing to me if my daughter didn't know I loved her.

Money isn't *everything*, but it isn't *nothing* either. I wouldn't want to trade places with an impoverished man with prospects either. The Buddha taught me how to have a healthy relationship with money, wealth, and greed amidst the materialistic chaos not just on the trading floor, but in the modern world.

But none of this meant anything to me when I was growing up in a Northern California suburb of Sacramento in the 1980's.

As a kid, I rejected austerity just as Siddhartha had, although in my case I rejected it without consideration. Like every American kid in the 1980's, I did not reject luxury and wealth, I worshiped it. I wanted to drive a car like Sonny Crockett, live in a house like J.R. Ewing, and succeed faster than Bud Fox. The only Buddha I knew was the fat statue that rested behind the bar at an all-you-can-eat Asian buffet restaurant near school where my high school football team liked to eat. So how did I get from worshipping Sonny Crocket to worshiping Buddha? Let's start with *my* "creation story."

Sacramento

The streets in suburban Sacramento are wide and clean, lined with well-tended lawns and only an occasional car parked along the curb. I loved pedaling my bike alone through the ordered stillness of the well-planned streets. When I was growing up, the family television drama "Eight Is Enough" was set in Sacramento and typified the culture there. Nice, but dull. Suburban. I imagined the limitless and amazing things I would do if I lived in a city like New York or San Francisco. Or how I would be "country strong" – living on a ranch in the countryside, able to gallop a horse across the desert plains. I wished I lived ninety miles to our east, in Tahoe City, skiing year-round, carving fresh powder at Squaw Valley in the winter and jumping the boat's wake on Lake Tahoe in the summer. By the time I was twelve, I wished I lived *anywhere* else but in Sacramento.

The only thing that interested me about my town was the American River and the trails around it. I loved the hypnotic sound of the current, the fresh smell of the water, the sense of motion and life. We lived a few blocks from the river and I spent countless hours there. With a fishing pole strapped to my back and tackle in my pockets, I'd ride my bike over the levy and down the trails as far as I could before stashing it in the bushes and heading to the river. I would get as close as I could to the rapids, and spent hours watching them change, the water in constant motion, the river an immovable force.

In my youth, my favorite thing to do on the river was what we called "skim boarding." In a land-locked place like Sacramento, *skim boarding* is done on a river rapid, instead of the ocean's surf. All we needed was a piece of plywood, some rope and a garage door spring. The latter was the most difficult to procure (all of our parents got tired of having stretched garage door springs). We trimmed the plywood until it was roughly four feet long by three feet wide with a point at one end. Then we would drill a hole in the pointed end, cut a six-foot-long piece of rope and tie it in a loop through the hole to serve as a handle. Next, we tied one end of a fifty-foot long rope to the front to the board and to the garage door spring. We would take this contraption to one of our favorite rapids, find a tree just upstream and tie the other end of rope to it and to the unused end of the garage door spring. Then we would stretch the slack out of the long rope by walking down river until the rope was tight and we could feel the spring. Once the rope was stretched as far as we could pull it, we would jump on the board, balance using the handle, and move into the rapids by leaning out. It was a great feeling, like racing behind a boat and yet standing still. When we got older we learned to do tricks to entertain the passing rafters, hoping they might thank us by throwing us a beer.

I have always loved nature and our family spent nearly every vacation we took at Lake Tahoe. Tahoe remains heaven to me and I still feel a sense of wonder as I type the word now. The lake, in all its different moods, has always drawn me to it - a dark and mysterious lover in the winter and a vibrant sun-kissed mistress in the summer. Tahoe was the only vacation we ever took as a family and we usually stayed with our family friends the Grebituses (the same family my mentor hails from) at their cabin on the west shore.

One summer, I found an old broken down outboard motor in their garage and my Dad helped me get it running. We mounted it onto the little rowboat that we had on the beach. The motor was able to push the boat and me, but very slowly and very loudly. So much noise for so little power, but I found the steady hum soothing. I spent whole days in my "putt-putt" roaming the west shore of Lake Tahoe like a coast guard clipper on patrol.

My family was what I call "holiday Christians." We went to a couple of church services a year, usually around Christmas and Easter and said grace before dinner only for special events, holidays, and birthdays. From preschool through sixth grade my sister and I attended a small Episcopalian primary school called St. Michael's. My parents sent us there not out of devotion to the Episcopalian faith but because it offered a good education at a reasonable price.

St. Michael's was co-ed, but out of the twenty kids in my grade, only one was a girl. Colleen was a shy nerdy blonde with glasses who always looked as uncomfortable as she probably felt. She left the school after fourth grade, probably unable to take it any longer and finally doing whatever it took to convince her parents to send her to a different school. Just as were beginning to think about girls, dark-eyed, freckled Carrie joined our class in fifth grade. She was mysterious to us and seemed more mature. I wonder how she felt that first day of fifth grade, in a class full of boys, all of whom were in love with her, but none of whom were able to utter a word in her presence.

Every school day at St Michael's started with students lining up single file outside their classroom doors silently waiting to be told by the teachers to proceed into the chapel. The teachers marched us in by grade, with the youngest kids first so they could sit in the front pews with the older kids behind them. The minister would say a few prayers to the chapel full of yawning and lethargic six to twelve-year olds and then announce any special activities or schedules before releasing us by grade, in the same order, to go to our classrooms. Like most of the kids in our school, I stayed as close to sleep throughout this entire process as I could.

Part of our schoolwork was a Bible Studies class on Thursday afternoons, taught by our Headmaster, Father Paul Christenson or "Father Paul" as we called him. Father Paul arrived at St Michaels when I was in fourth grade. He had jet-black hair, wore stylish rimmed glasses and seemed more modern and less anachronistic than the other ministers at the parish. As a result, I became more interested in the Bible Studies class than I had been when Father Paul's predecessor, who looked 150 years old and smelled of camphor, taught it.

On the way home from one our infrequent visits to church I asked my parents why we didn't go more often.

"We go plenty often," was my mother's dismissive reply.

"Aren't we supposed to go every Sunday?" I asked.

"Who says we are *supposed* to?" my mom asked.

"God," I said. "In the Bible."

"Well, God understands we are a busy family," she said, hoping to end the conversation.

But now that I was paying more attention in bible studies, I was becoming disturbed by what we were being taught. The God I heard about from my parents and during the few Sunday school classes we attended was kind, loving, benevolent…not the God of the Old Testament. Reading the story of Noah and the flood, I did think it was good that God saved Noah, his wife and family, and two of every animal; but I was distraught that it also meant he had killed every other person and creature in the world, innocent or guilty, young and old.

"…all flesh died that moved on earth, birds, domestic animals, wild animals, all swarming creatures that swarm on the earth, and all human beings; everything on dry land in whose nostrils was the breath of life died." (Genesis 7:21-22)

Even if I could have believed that every human being (except for one family) had sinned enough to somehow deserve death, as an animal lover, the image of an innocent horse being swept up in an ever-rising tide, unable to swim, terrified and drowning, was deeply troubling to me.

In Exodus, God brings ten plagues upon the Egyptians because their Pharaoh won't release the Jews from slavery. I agreed that slavery is bad, and I was happy that God saved the Jews from it, but, again, the methods seemed indiscriminate. The ten plagues God sent to punish the Pharaoh were horrific and torturous, and again punished not just the offender but also all Egyptians, many of whom were already suffering at the hand of their leader. God turned all water into blood, released a swarm of frogs, followed by a swarm of lice, and then a swarm of flies on all of Egypt. When the Pharaoh's heart was still hardened, God struck all domestic animals in Egypt with a deadly pestilence. Still unsatisfied, God struck all the Egyptian people and their animals with boils. Then He sent thunder and hailstones big enough to kill men and animals, then locusts, then three days of darkness. Finally, in Exodus 12:29, he sent the tenth plague.

"At midnight the Lord struck down all firstborn in the land of Egypt, from the first born of the Pharaoh who sat on his throne to the firstborn of the prisoner who was in the dungeon, and all the firstborn of the livestock."

As terrible and unjust as all these things were, the thing that most disturbed me was what happened after the seventh plague. Exodus 10 1-2:

"Then the Lord said to Moses 'Go to Pharaoh; for I have hardened his heart and the hearts of his officials, in order that I may show these signs of mine among them, and that you may tell your children and grandchildren how I have made fools of the Egyptians and what signs I have done among them – so that you may know that I am the Lord.'"

I kept reading this over and over, but it seemed to say the same thing: After the first seven plagues, the Pharaoh actually capitulated to God's will but then God hardened the Egyptian's heart, and the hearts of those around him, forcing them to disobey Him so He could strike three more plagues on them to prove his power and strength to his followers. To my young mind, He was a bigger bully than I had ever faced on the playground. When I asked Father Paul about these stories, he was vague.

"God works in mysterious ways," he'd say cryptically.

Lying in bed at night imagining the drowning horses, the innocent plague-stricken Egyptian farmers and their livestock, I would try to make sense of Father Paul's explanation, but it didn't seem very mysterious to me. Cruelty and unfairness weren't a mystery, they were just wrong. When I got older, I came to interpret these stories as literary expressions, but my young mind was righteous and extremely indignant. I decided I could not worship the God I was reading about at St. Michael's.

One night, when I was ten-years old, we sat down to dinner and I made an announcement.

"I'm not going to church with you all on Sundays," I said. "And I am not going to morning chapel at school either. I don't believe in God and I don't think I should go if I don't believe."

My sister, Georgiana, who had just graduated from St Michaels and who had attended church every morning during her seven years there was the first to react.

"No way," she said. "You're not getting out of it that easy! Mom? DAD?"

"Calm down," my mom told her. "Of course Robert will be attending morning chapel and joining us when we attend church."

My mother wasn't particularly devout but she certainly didn't want an *atheist* for a son.

With a nervous laugh she added, "I've never heard such a thing!"

"No, I'm not going to go," I replied. "You're supposed to *believe* in God and Jesus if you go and I don't."

"You do so believe in God," Mom said. "Don't say that! Do you want to rot in h-e-double toothpicks?"

"I don't believe in H-E- double toothpicks anymore," I said, afraid to say the word "hell" whether I believed in it or not.

My mother looked like she was going to rain fire and brimstone down on me like a fundamentalist preacher at a gay wedding. But just before she could start, my dad spoke up.

"Why don't we set up a meeting with your headmaster?" Dad said. "Father Paul, isn't it? We can all discuss this together."

As it was in most families at that time, my father was not actually asking a question nor was he expecting an answer.

On the appointed day the following week, after school ended, instead of heading out to find the parent driving carpool that day, I said goodbye to my friends and headed back toward the chapel where the school offices were. I crept through the small school library, as empty as it always was, to get to the headmaster's office. When I opened the door, I saw my parents sitting patiently, eyes straight ahead, on the long bench usually occupied by students awaiting punishment for some schoolyard or classroom offense. Mom looked like just being there on the bench was a worse punishment than what the usual occupiers of her seat feared. I hung my head miserable knowing *I* was the reason the three of us were on the bench today. As my head spun with regret, the school secretary, Mrs. Harris, invited us to join Father Paul in his office.

Father Paul stood and greeted us warmly when we walked in. He offered Mom and Dad the two chairs opposite his desk and told me to stand behind them. I hovered uncomfortably there, not sure exactly where or how to stand, and looked around the room for somewhere to comfortably rest my eyes. Father Paul welcomed us again and Dad started by explaining my position on church attendance. As soon as he finished, and before the headmaster could reply, Mom started to describe her concern for my eternal soul, but finally, Father Paul interrupted her.

"If Robert is questioning his faith and feels uncomfortable in morning chapel he can be excused from attending," he said.

"He will still, of course, need to complete his Bible Studies class," he said to my parents. Then he looked me squarely in the eye and said, "Robert, I hope you will keep your heart open to Jesus Christ, whether you take him as your savior or not."

My mother looked like a woman who had just been told the sky is green and trees are purple. She began making small noises, starting words she was unable to finish, then she nervously fidgeted while desperately looking around for someone to tell her this was all a joke. Dad, sensing Mom might start finishing her words and fearing what they might be, wrapped it up.

"Thanks, Father Paul," Dad said. "I need to get these two home and then get back to the office."

With that, he had Mom by her hand and we were headed for the car in the now nearly empty playground parking lot.

"I hope you're happy," was all Mom said to me for the rest of the day.

Mom and Dad

My father was born in Sacramento to an Irish mother and a Greek father who ran a dry-cleaning shop on X Street in a bad neighborhood on the edge of downtown. Dad and his sister, Irene, had a difficult childhood. Their mother, who had been sick throughout her life, and spent time in a sanitarium in Grass Valley, California, died shortly after giving birth to my father. My grandfather quickly remarried, this time to a greek woman named Katrina, who was abusive to my Dad. I've never known what form the abuse took, only that my mother, who never said anything negative about anybody, said it was too horrible to describe. Mom referred to Katrina as "that vile woman." My grandfather was emotionally absent and unavailable.

I was terrified of going to Grandpa and Katrina's house. It was like travelling back in time to a foreign land, unlike anything I knew. Even the homemade Greek candies they offered my sister and me were too strange to enjoy. There wasn't a comfortable place to sit in the entire house - it was the only home I had ever seen with plastic covers on all the furniture. Furthermore, Grandpa spoke to us in Greek which we didn't understand. It sounded distant and angry to my sister and me. Grandpa and Katrina were Greek Orthodox Christians and seemed to assume we were too, and Dad never disabused them of it. But the scariest part was watching my dad around his father. Uneasy and anxious to avoid confrontation, Dad spoke to his father in a tone of voice we never heard his use anywhere else.

Although I knew Katrina was not my natural grandmother, because she and Grandpa were *so* Greek, I assumed my natural grandmother was also Greek, and that I was, therefore, half Greek. I never questioned this ethnicity until, when I was in my thirties, my mother casually mentioned my "Irish grandmothers" for the first time.

"*Grandmother* you mean?" I said, changing the plural to singular. I knew my mom's mother, born Edna Kennedy, was Irish.

"No, grandmothers," Mom said, emphasizing the *s*. "Your Dad's mother's side was Irish, too. When your grandfather married outside the Greek Orthodox Church it caused a huge scandal. They were never accepted. That's why he married Katrina so quickly after...."

She continued, but I had stopped listening. All my life I had defined myself as mostly Greek, told people I was Greek, and firmly (and proudly?) believed I had the ethnic characteristics of a Greek. But I was, in fact, not half-Greek, but half-Irish. Irish not Greek. Whiskey not ouzo, Joyce not Plato, the Emerald Isle not the Olympic Peninsula. My entire self-identity shifted beneath me.

Both Grandpa and Katrina died in my childhood. I remember attending my grandfather's funeral in a Greek Orthodox church when I was nine. The church was dark and unbelievably somber, all the light swallowed by a void. The ceremony, performed in Greek, was so strange that it felt to me more like a satanic ritual than a Christian funeral. The casket was open and I couldn't take my eyes off my grandfather's body, dressed in a suit, with the same stern expression he had always worn in life. He looked like he might stand up and start talking to me in Greek. The service reminded me of him; austere and stern, dark, incomprehensible, and separate from the world I inhabited.

My mom's father, William LeNoir, was by all accounts, a kind and generous man. He was a painter and was commissioned by the state of California to paint scenes from the state's past and some of them still hang in the California State Capitol building. He died when I was very young and I have no actual memories of him, just stories I have heard, and some of his paintings hanging in my house.

All of my memories of my mother's mother are after she started living in a place called the Pioneer House. The Pioneer House is what we now call an *assisted living facility* but was known then as *the old folk's home*. Just as I dreaded the prospect of visiting Grandpa and Katrina's house, I dreaded our occasional visits to the Pioneer House.

As a kid, I played little league baseball and youth basketball and flag football. I learned to waterski and snow-ski and to play golf and tennis from my dad. I liked sports and was naturally good at most of them, though not great at anyone in particular. My father helped, supported, and coached me in many of my athletic activities and rarely missed one of my games.

An accomplished and competitive skier, golfer, and tennis player Dad made his living as a ski instructor and golf pro when he was a young man. But when he married Mom he settled down and got a job selling cars at Hubacher Cadillac, a dealership in Sacramento. Later, he became a stockbroker and did well for a while primarily because of one large client, Dr. Roy Jones. Dr. Jones was a wealthy doctor from an old San Francisco family, and he was impressed with my dad when Dad cold-called him at his ranch in Marysville, California. Without Dr. Jones's business, my dad would not have been able to make a living as a stockbroker. With it, we lived a comfortable, if simple, suburban life.

I loved all the sports my dad did and we spent a lot of time together golfing, skiing, playing tennis, and fishing. Like most boys my age, I wanted to do everything my father did and nothing he didn't. But in fourth grade, quite unexpectedly, I decided I wanted to play soccer. Nobody I knew played, we didn't even own a soccer ball, and I had never seen a game. Pele had just come to play in New York and the US Soccer League (USSL) was trying to break into the American sports consciousness and I guess it worked on me. When I told my father I wanted to play soccer, he found a local team, signed me up, and started kicking a ball back and forth with me in our yard.

But we were late signing up and the team was full. The league told us that there were enough kids that hadn't made the first team to form a second team but that they didn't have anyone to coach it. Despite having kicked a soccer ball for the first time only days earlier, Dad volunteered on the spot. That night he went to a local sporting goods store, bought a pair of soccer cleats, a ball, a whistle, an official American Youth Soccer Rulebook, and signed up for a coaching class at Sacramento State University.

On the first day of practice, it was obvious why most of our players had been cut from the "A" team: we were a sorry group of uninspired scrappy misfits. More than half the kids were on the team only because their parents were making them play a sport and soccer was the least threatening. Despite my complete lack of experience, my slightly above-average athletic ability made me the best player on our poor team. And although Dad was a quick study and soon became a good coach, we lost nearly every game, rarely scoring and often never getting out of our own half with the ball. In our first game I played striker, our best and only hope to score, but I spent the entire game watching the other team attack our defense and score. By the second game, I moved to central defender so I could at least slow the bleeding.

A few weeks into the season, Coach Garcia, the coach of the A team, called my dad and asked if I would like to fill in for them. His team was short a player for their weekend game. The A game was in the morning so I would still be able play for our B team in the afternoon. I was thrilled to get to play two games in one day.

I played both games and, although it exhausted me, I loved it. Early in the first game, Coach Garcia yelled at me for drifting out of position and I felt my cheeks blush. I was happy to redeem myself in the second half by passing well, scoring a goal, and making an important defensive interception. I'd played my best game yet, clearly improved and inspired by the experience of playing with better teammates. After our game, I saw Coach Garcia talking to my dad but I was off with the team eating orange slices and drinking Hi-C punch brought by the team mom, so I couldn't hear their conversation.

Then we got home.

"Come in and sit down," Dad said to me. "We have something we need to talk about."

As it would any kid, this put a pit in the middle of my stomach. I tried to remember if I had done anything bad or forgotten to do something - anything that would get me in trouble. I couldn't think of any recent indiscretion, but I knew there had to be some. I sat down nervously and waited for Dad, who had gone into the kitchen and was pouring himself some iced tea.

Finally, he came back in and sat down.

"Coach Garcia from the A team has invited you to join their team for the rest of the season," he said.

Initially I felt relieved I was not in trouble. I started breathing again. My stomach unclenched. Then I felt elated, thrilled to get to play for the better team and for my dad's team. But, before I could say anything, he added,

"You would have to quit our team though," he said, as if reading my mind. "You can't play for two different teams more than once."

My stomach tightened again and my head started spinning. I felt torn in half. I wanted to play on the A team with the better players (and win some games!) but I also liked playing for my dad.

Dad could see my ambivalence.

"Whenever I have a difficult decision to make," he said, "I take a piece of paper and I draw a line down the middle of it. Then I write the reasons in favor of each choice on opposite sides of the line. Why don't you try that?"

With that, he got up and went to the sliding glass door that opened onto our back yard. Just before he slid the door shut behind him, he turned back to me.

"I want you to know," he said, "I'll be perfectly happy whatever you decide."

Alone in the house, the stillness was complete. I got up, went to the desk and took out a blank piece of paper and a pencil. I sat down at our dining table and drew a line down the middle of the page and wrote "A Team" on the left and "Dad's Team" on the right. I started on the left side and wrote:

"Play with the best players."

"Play Striker."

"Score goals."

"Play on a better team."

"Win lots of games."

"Get better at the sport."

"Win some tournaments."

"Play more games."

On the right side of the paper, I wrote three words.

"Play for Dad."

I tried to think of other reasons to put in Dad's column but couldn't. I sat staring at the lopsided list, the lone reason on the right glaring up at me like a kid not picked for the game at recess. I crumpled up the paper, threw it in the trashcan, stood up, and headed out to the back yard to tell my dad what I decided. I walked across our small lawn to where he was trimming a hedge.

"I'm gonna play for you," I said.

He continued working, pausing just for one beat as I spoke, and nodding solumnly like I was telling him something he already knew.

 While my father was a typical American dad -- helped me with sports, did projects with me, and nurtured me into manhood -- my mom was an atypical mom. She was not nurturing or motherly in traditional ways (though she loved us in her way). I believe she never really wanted kids, only capitulating after all her friends did. Mom and Dad had been married for ten years and were in their late-thirties when they finally had my sister, Georgiana, and then, nineteen months later, me.

Mom was a pure optimist. She didn't see the glass as half full or half empty, she was just thrilled to have some water. Whenever she called me, she always asked the same question.

"How are things?" she'd ask, but before waiting for answer she'd always add, "good?"

Inquiring about me while directing my response. She was great to talk to when things were going well, marveling at my accomplishments and telling me how smart I was. I loved her for it. Everyone should be lucky enough to have someone as blindly supportive and positive. She wasn't, however, able to hear bad news nor was she able to respond to bad news in a thoughtful or supportive way. It just made her anxious and depressed. If I were to answer her question by saying, "actually, I'm not that good, Mom -- I lost a bunch of money on a bad trade yesterday," she would say something like,

"Well, I'm sure you'll figure it all out."

Then she wouldn't speak of it again for months until, after a few glasses of wine one night, she would burst out crying.

"Are you completely broke?" she'd implore. "Is your business bankrupt? We can sell the house, you know. I'm so worried about you!"

But usually by then, the crisis had long passed and more likely than not I'd forgotten about the bad trade but nevertheless, I'd have to spend the rest of the evening reassuring her.

Mom was diagnosed with breast cancer when I was ten-years old. After a mastectomy, she was put on chemotherapy and radiation, which was even more physically devastating back in the late 1970's than it is now. Though I didn't know it at the time, the doctor told my dad that she would not live more than six months after the date of diagnosis.

I don't remember many details from our many hospital visits nor do I recall the effects treatment had on her nor that my sister was too scared to visit Mom in the hospital and stayed home (she told me this years later). I do, however, vividly remember sitting in a doctor's office with my dad and being intimidated when the somber doctor addressed me.

"Your mom has cancer," he spoke in the stern way grown-ups who don't have kids speak to kids. "Now, we've taken most of it out and your mother is taking medicine to get the rest. She's going to need all her strength in order to recover so you need to be a good little boy and not upset her."

From then on, even after the cancer was gone, I did whatever I could to keep my mom happy and relaxed. To be a *good little boy*. I showed her only the parts of my life that were likely to please her and never mentioned any of my struggles. I became her emotional caregiver. It worked out very well; I was good at caregiving and she was good at care-receiving. I didn't have to stick to the truth to make her happy, she did not scrutinize things that pleased her, and I framed the world in wonder and goodness. *Everything's fine*, I'd tell Mom. *Everything's great.*

When she talked about the cancer, my mother acted like it was a small, temporary inconvenience -- more like a sprained joint or a strained muscle than a terminal illness. If anyone asked how she was doing she would invariably say,

"I'm fine! I am perfectly fine, thank you very much."

As a young boy, I didn't know much about cancer and accepted my parents story that, though Mom was sick, she would be fine in a few months when the treatments were completed. I was doing as the doctor told me, making sure my sister and I were well-behaved, or at least covert in our misbehavior, and anyway, Mom kept saying she was fine so, in time, I believed her.

Then, one day at school, I was talking with my classmates, listing facts about parents like kids do.

"My mom has cancer," I said, believing it to be just another silly fact like "my dad sells insurance" or "my mom plays tennis."

"She has *cancer*?" a kid named Todd Wilson said, his eyes wide open in near disbelief. "She's gonna *die*!"

"No, she's not," I yelled at Todd. "She's already mostly better!"

"No, she's gonna die," Todd insisted. He turned so the other kids could hear him. "Cancer kills people!"

We were quickly on the ground, rolling around, exhausted and holding onto each other's arms more than trying to get our own loose for punching.

"Fight, fight, fight," the kids chanted as they formed a circle around us. When the teacher arrived to break us up I was relieved. I'd been too tired to land a blow and was afraid Todd, the bigger boy, might get one in on me. The teacher had separated us just in time. He took us each by the arm and marched us directly to the headmaster's office.

We could feel Father Paul's disappointment, and that disappointment was the worst punishment of all. He never asked what the fight was about and I don't know if he knew, he just told us fighting was not Christian and not accepted at St. Michael's and then sent us both home for the rest of the day.

Though cancer does kill a lot of people, especially back then, it didn't kill my mother. Her doctor credited her optimism for beating the terminal diagnosis, saying the fact that Mom never even considered that she might not survive ended up saving her life. He recalled the day he first explained Mom's bleak diagnosis to her.

"I am sure you are a very good doctor," Mom had told her doctor that first day. "But *you are wrong about this*, doctor."

Dad was diagnosed with adult onset diabetes in his early forties. It was routine for me to watch him take out a hypodermic needle, fill it from one of the small vials of insulin he kept in the refrigerator door, and inject it into his leg before breakfast. Insulin is the enzyme that regulates sugar in our bodies – an enzyme a diabetic's body can't sufficiently produce. The injection processes excess sugar for the diabetic, keeping the level of sugar in their bloodstream in a healthy range. Sometimes, the insulin works too well and destroys all the sugar in the bloodstream, leaving the patient weak and dizzy, and, if they do not get sugar into their bloodstream quickly, in a coma or dead. This is called "Diabetic Shock" or an "Insulin Reaction." For this reason, Dad kept an emergency stash of candy bars in our house.

One day, my mom saw me gazing longingly at the candy stash.

"If you eat Dad's candy," she said, "and he has an insulin reaction, *he'll die*."

I never touched the candy.

For ten years after his diagnosis, Dad managed the diabetes well and was able to maintain an active lifestyle. We still skied, biked, hiked and played golf together frequently.

Then, early one Sunday morning, we were playing as a twosome at Haggin Oaks, a public golf course in North Sacramento. As we approached the sixth green, we split up; Dad walked to the left side to chip his ball and I walked over the green to the right where my ball had landed. I found it, selected a club, and looked over to see if Dad had taken his shot. I couldn't see him.

"Dad?" I called.

No answer.

I jogged back onto the green but I still couldn't see him.

"Dad?" I called louder. "Did you find your ball?"

Still no response so I started quickly across the green to the side he had been on. As I came over the crest of the green I saw my father slumped on the ground, balanced awkwardly on hand and hip, his bag laying on the grass next to him, his clubs spilling out of it.

For a few seconds I froze.

I couldn't breathe and it felt as if my heart had stopped beating. I dropped my club and ran as fast as I could to him, sliding in on a knee to stop myself next to him. He was nearly unconscious and could only manage a single word.

"Sugar," he whispered.

I turned to his bag, where he often had a candy bar stashed, but before I could reach it he managed another word.

"No."

He had nothing in his bag.

I looked around but we were a long way from the clubhouse, too far for me to run there and back. I saw a cart parked at the next tee and without thinking, ran to it, jumped in, and raced it back to Dad. I somehow managed to get him in the passenger seat where he slumped forward. I ran around to the driver's side, helped him sit back, wrapped my right arm around tightly around his midsection to hold him in the cart. I slammed the pedal into the floor and drove as fast as I could to the clubhouse, crossing fairways that golfers were hitting into. I didn't hear anyone yelling at me for stealing their cart (and their clubs), though I am sure they did.

At the clubhouse, I ran in, grabbed a Hershey chocolate bar and told the woman at the counter I'd be right back. Then I ran back out to my dad. Hands shaking, I took the candy out of the wrapper and broke off a big piece. I held it out to him but he just opened his mouth so I put it directly in his mouth. He was too weak to chew, instead he closed his mouth and let it melt and swallowed.

The effect was immediate.

His eyes were back in focus and his strength returned as if a magic wand had been waved. Dad sat up, took a deep breath, and shook his arms out. He looked at me and asked:

"Did you pay for the candy bar?"

He was fine. I was not. My hands were shaking for the rest of the day.

His body held up through the first ten years of my life but ultimately, he couldn't avoid the devastating side effects of the disease. When he was coaching the State Farm Tigers, my Senior Farm Little League team, he developed calcium deposits in his shoulders. The deposits were painful and limited his range of motion so he couldn't throw or hit the baseball without discomfort. It made him throw "like a girl," swinging the bat awkwardly, wincing in pain. My teammates were, of course, ruthless about it. They made fun of his movements and did impressions behind his back (and sometimes mine) of the faces he made. If an errant throw came at him and he had to react quickly to reach it, he would get shooting pains that caused him to wince and make strange faces. I was horrified to see it; not because he was in pain, but because he was *embarrassing me*.

The shame I felt for my dad at practice was crippling, but it was surpassed by the fear I felt afterward, a fear that my father had sensed that I was ashamed of him. I swore to myself I would stand up to my teammates. I would make them stop mocking him. I would get into a fight if I had to. I even knew which teammate I would have to fight. Billy Sargent was our ace pitcher and best hitter. He played shortstop on the days he didn't pitch but whatever position he played, he hit cleanup and was our best overall player. He was also the ringleader of the boys who mocked my dad.

My resolve weakened, however, when I got to practice. My overwhelming need to fit in with my teammates took over and I knew beating up our best player wasn't going to help. I was a shy kid, but I usually was able to fit into a group, especially a sports team. The problem was, they didn't want to make fun of my dad in front of me but they did want to make fun of him. All the time.

Finally, I figured out how to fix it. At the time I thought it, my idea seemed brilliant to me. I was working out with the pitchers and infielders in left field while my dad stood near home plate hitting fly balls to the outfielders gathered in right field. Trying to hit one over our centerfielder's head, Dad swung too hard and winced in pain and spun around holding his shoulder. I was with Billy Sargent and a bunch of my teammates in left field staring at Dad, watching him suffer.

Then I did it.

I yelped in mock pain and twisted my face into a grimace, spinning around in imitation of my father. Actually, for dramatic effect, I made it worse than it was, yelping like a baby and dramatically spinning around grasping my shoulder. When I finished, there was complete silence. My teammates looked at me like I was some kind of monster. I felt so ashamed I couldn't even look over at my father.

I had no way of knowing it but Dad's health problems were only just beginning. His diabetes caused poor circulation, which shot pain down his legs and made his fingers and toes numb. When he was working ski patrol in Sun Valley, Idaho, as a young man, Dad broke his foot at the beginning of the season but, unable to afford not working, he skied on it all year. By the time he got it set, some permanent damage had been done and it bothered him for the rest of his life. Well, at least until his poor circulation forced him to have it amputated. He came home from the hospital wearing a cast on his left leg with only a small ball where his ankle and foot should have been - a modern peg-legged pirate.

For six months, while the leg healed, he hobbled around with a cane. During this time, Dad needed to visit Dr. Jones in San Francisco to get his signature on some documents and, although he could drive around town albeit awkwardly, I had recently gotten my driver's license so Dad asked me to drive. We briefly visited Dr. Jones at his house and got the signatures. I was in awe of doctor's beautiful house with its amazing views of San Francisco.

Afterward, we drove to the Hippopotamus restaurant on Van Ness Avenue to get hamburgers before we drove home. Now defunct, the Hippo was a popular spot back then and there was a wait for a table so we put our name on the list and found seats in the waiting area, across from a young family. Their young son was staring at the bottom of Dad's cast. Then I saw his mother had noticed him staring, but he got the words out before she could stop him.

"Hey mister," the little boy asked. "What happened to your foot?"

It felt like all the activity in the busy restaurant came to complete stop, the boy's parents looked horrified like they were witnessing a car accident they couldn't prevent. My heart stopped and I, along with everyone else, looked at my Dad.

Without missing a beat and before the boy's parents could apologize, my dad kindly spoke to the curious kid.

"Thanks for asking," he said. "I broke it a long time ago and didn't take good care of it so it had to be cut off. My leg is still healing but pretty soon I'll get this cast off and they will give ne a new foot."

"A *new foot*?" the boy's eyes were wide with amazement.

My dad chuckled before replying.

"Well, it's a fake foot," he said, "but I'll be good as new, don't you worry."

He paused and the horrified parents thought the awkward situation was over, but then Dad turned to the boy again.

"What's your name?" he asked.

"Michael," the boy replied.

"Do you want to feel the end of my cast, Michael?" Dad held up his peg leg.

The boy looked hopefully at his parents, sensing he would need their permission. Just then, the restaurant called his family's name and his relieved parents hurriedly dragged him away, apologizing to Dad over their shoulders until they were out of sight.

"Nice kid," was all my father said to me.

Once the wound healed, Dad wore his prosthetic foot and was able to get around pretty well. He even managed to play golf for a few more years. He played long after his legs got weaker with phlebitis (blood clots) and he had to use a golf cart to get around. We played together until he could no longer see the ball well enough to hit it. Still, despite his many maladies, I never beat him.

Dad's health continued to decline through my years in high school. We opened presents one Christmas morning in a semi-private hospital room, crowded on our side of the curtain, keeping our voices down for the patient on the other side who had no visitors. Not long after that, Dad's kidneys began to fail and he required dialysis twice a week. His eyesight deteriorated despite several surgeries.

Dad's commission income declined along with his health. Dr. Jones passed away, leaving his fortune to his children, all of whom had to their own advisors. Other clients got frustrated when he wasn't in the office to take their calls and switched to another broker. The only clients who stayed with him were his friends, and even they started taking their accounts away. Dad's income decreased almost as quickly as the medical expenses increased, and by the time I was applying to colleges our family finances were dire, so I planned a way to finance my own education. I applied for state and federal grants, took out student loans, and planned to work as much as possible.

The one thing that my dad always insisted on was me going to college. Dad never had the opportunity to go to college; he joined the Navy to fight in World War II on his eighteenth birthday. A few months prior he had been involved in a bar brawl and found himself in front of a judge, charged with assault. The judge gave him a choice between jail and the military. He chose the Navy and served in Guam until the end of the war. When he was discharged, he moved to Lake Tahoe with his friend, Dick Buek, where they both worked on the ski patrol at Soda Springs and Sugar Bowl. It never occurred to me that many GI's entered universities when they returned from the war and that Dad had instead chosen to ski, so saying he never had the chance to get a degree was not altogether true.

Mom had spent a few semesters at the University of California at Berkeley before dropping out to work in a typing pool at the state capitol in Sacramento. My sister's college career consisted of one semester at a local junior college. I was our only hope. I never questioned the path my dad laid out for me: elementary school, middle school, high school, get into a good university, earn a degree, get an important job.

I loved playing football. I was six-foot-one and weighed two-hundred and twenty-five pounds by my senior year of high school, and up to 260 pounds in college. I lifted weights and trained six days a week throughout high school and was starting on the varsity offensive line as a sophomore. I played both offensive and defensive lines as a junior and senior. The physicality and violence of the game made me feel alive. When I was on the field, I always knew what to do and the struggle was physical.

I was recruited as an offensive lineman. In high school I had played everywhere on the offensive line, but colleges were attracted by my quickness and wanted me as a pulling guard. I was the biggest guy on my high school team but would be one of the smaller lineman on a college team. I decided to visit two of the schools recruiting me in order to choose between them. The first, the University of California at Davis (UC Davis), was a good public university and a Division II football powerhouse - they had won their division, they held the NCAA record sixteen years in a row. And it was only a half an hour from my parent's house.

My official visit was to begin with a tour of campus at 11:00 in the morning but I arrived an hour early to get a feel of the school on my own. Though I'd grown up so close campus, I'd never been on it before. UC Davis has large agriculture and veterinary schools and detractors would always joke about the smell on campus. As soon as I opened my car door, I realized that this wasn't just a joke. It smelled like the inside of a barn.

At 11:00, I was led, along with a few other recruits, on a tour of the campus. Our guide was a sweet and flirty senior named Sarah. She told us everything you could possibly want to know about the school, but never once did she mention the smell. We ate lunch at the student union with some UC Davis players who had grown up in Sacramento. We talked about the high schools we had played for and compared successes. When I mentioned that my team was 2-9 my senior season, they laughed.

"You're in the right place," one of them said.

After lunch it was finally time for my one-one one meeting with Head Coach Jim Sochor. I had heard that Sochor was a Buddhist but aback then I had no idea what that really meant. Coach Sochor was the first Buddhist I ever met. After a brief wait, his secretary told me to go into his office, where the coach sitting comfortably behind his desk, looking out the window, past swim practice in the pool, to the sky. It was a brilliant late winter day and he kept staring silently out the window after I sat down. Finally, he looked at me.

"I love this time of year," he said, motioning to the window and the beautiful weather on the other side of it. "You can smell the new beginnings."

Unsure how to reply, although oddly moved by the comment, I simply said, "Me too, Coach."

We talked about campus a little as he prepared the film projector to show me a play from the previous season. In it, Davis is on offense and the star quarterback, Scott Barry, rolls out to his left and looks downfield. Unable to find an open receiver, he runs to the sideline and is shoved out of bounds by a linebacker. But before he can slow his momentum, Barry runs into a cheerleader from the opposing school and they both to tumble to the ground. The cheerleader rolls over and sits up uninjured but obviously shaken. Barry scrambles to his feet and hurries back to the huddle. Coach stopped the film.

"See that?" he asks. "He should've stopped right there and helped the young lady to her feet. Where else would you knock someone down and just run away? That's a missed opportunity."

Again unsure how to reply, I just nodded my head.

The secretary opened the door, signifying my time was up and the next recruit was ready to enter. Coach Sochor smiled, shook my hand, and said he hoped to see me in August.

I thanked him and left.

Other than this strangely enjoyable meeting with the Buddhist coach, the most memorable part of the visit was the *stench* that hung in the air everywhere on campus.

My second visit was to California Polytechnic University (nicknamed Cal Poly) in San Louis Obispo. Cal Poly was another good California public university. Driving my sister's beat-up Volkswagen three hundred miles down the coast to San Luis Obispo, I felt alive and full of hope. I exited the freeway and drove into downtown SLO, a charming and historic southern California beach town. I found the campus, hilly and green, shining in the afternoon sun. I drove to the athletic facility, got out of the car and breathed in the fresh ocean air before heading into the coach's office.

The offensive coordinator, Coach Gross, welcomed me and asked if I liked what I'd seen of the town and campus. Although I could tell he knew the answer already, I told him I did. He gave me a tour of the sports facilities: the locker room, weight room, the practice field and finally, the stadium. All were newer and nicer than what I had seen at Davis. We finished the tour back at the office where we met a group of players talking with some other recruits. Coach assigned each recruit a player/chaperone. Mine was a sophomore quarterback from East Los Angeles named Robert Perez, and Robert Perez was the coolest kid I had ever met.

We went with two other recruits to a house just off-campus, where eight members of the football team lived and where they were barbequing what looked like a hundred pounds of steak and hamburger. We ate and met the players, who looked the other way when we filled our cups with beer. After dinner, girls started arriving. Then more girls. I spent the rest of the evening watching girls vie for players' attention, while the players drank beer and discussed where the surf would be best that weekend. I felt like I was in a dream and couldn't wait to make it reality the following year.

The next day I had lunch with a few of the coaches and two other recruits in the Faculty Dining Room. A high-ceilinged circular building with tall windows on top of a hill in the center of campus, it was beautiful and full of natural light. I felt grown-up as the coaches explained why I (and the other two recruits) should attend Cal Poly. The menus were printed on a small piece of paper and were only for the day. I looked at mine and saw it offered only three choices: some kind of salad, some kind of fish, or something I'd never heard of called a Monte Christo sandwich. I didn't like fish, and couldn't order a salad, so I ordered the Monte Christo.

When the food arrived, I looked at mine. It was a stack of French toast, not a sandwich.

"Uhh, I didn't want French toast," I stammered to the server. "I ordered the sandwich."

"Yes, the Monte Cristo," he said. "That's it, sir."

When I looked more closely, I saw it was filled with ham and melted cheese -- a *deep-fried* sandwich made with French toast bread. My cheeks flushed and I was sure everyone at the table was looking at me, pitying the hick from Sacramento. But embarrassment couldn't dampen my happiness.

Leaving San Luis Obispo that evening for the five-hour drive home, I felt ecstatic imagining I would be returning for school there in the fall. After lunch, I had even told the coaches that I planned to attend, explaining I'd accept formally once I talked to my parents. Pulling on to the coastal highway heading northbound, I pushed in the Who cassette tape I'd brought for the trip, *Who's Next,* and turned on the car stereo.

Triumphantly punching the air to the beats as I drove, I turned the volume all the way up for the *Baba O'Riley (Teenage Wasteland)* interlude, but when the drums exploded at the end of the song, as if synchronized, a small tuft of smoke rose from the dashboard and the stereo died. I heard the engine humming as the smoke cleared and I knew the sound of that engine would be the only sound I'd hear for the next five hours.

I drove north swimming in dreams of life at Cal Poly -- the town! the ocean! the fresh scent! After about an hour, I left the coast and cut over into the valley as it grew dark. My daydreams faded with the light; and my thoughts finally settled on my parents.

Though my mother wouldn't admit it, the strain of working full-time as well as taking care of Dad was taking a toll on my mom. And although *he* wouldn't admit it, Dad was lonely, trapped in a deteriorating body with little eyesight, and ever more dependent on Mom.

Driving for the next few hours, I tried to push everything out of my mind and rode in silence. By the time I exited Interstate 5 in Sacramento for the short drive to my parent's house, I knew I would be going to UC Davis. There hadn't been a moment of decision; I hadn't made a choice, I just knew I would. I didn't tell my parents much about my trip to San Luis Obispo, just that I had decided to go to UC Davis. They say after a couple of weeks you don't notice the smell anymore.

I spent my last summer in Sacramento working as many hours as I could get, training for football, and helping my parents sell our house, buy a condominium, and move into it. I was sad to see the house I'd lived in since sixth grade sold; but my parents could neither afford nor maintain it anymore. The proceeds paid off most of their medical bills and bought them a one-bedroom condominium a few miles away. In late July, I moved my stuff out of our old house and into my old Ford Escort. I spent my last few weeks in Sacramento sleeping on friend's couches.

Davis

I will never forget my first hit in college football. It was the third day of camp, but the first "full contact" session. We had spent the first few days walking through plays and doing non-contact drills, all the while sizing one another up. I wasn't the biggest or the fastest, but I knew my legs were strong and I had great technique. I had made a couple of All City, All-Star teams despite playing for a losing team and I knew I could hit. I was excited to test myself against my new teammates.

After calisthenics, the team broke up into position groups. The offensive linemen ran with a little extra intensity to our corner of the field. Coach had two of the older players demonstrate the first hitting drill. Player faced each other in three-point stances. On the coach's whistle, the players pulled and ran in the same direction, away from the line of scrimmage, before turning back up field and violently colliding at appointed spots.

I was lined up against Steve Jones, a junior and our starting right guard. He was big, but not one of the biggest guys, and was the clown of the group, so initially, even though I was facing a starter in my first college drill, I felt okay. I got into my three-point stance and waited what seemed like minutes not seconds for the whistle to blow. When it did, I leapt out of my stance, pulled as deep as I could, turned toward Steve, got low and slammed into him with all my strength. In high school, when I hit someone like this, the next thing to do was help him up. After colliding with Steve, however, I learned what it felt like to *get* hit. I was knocked back and struggled to stay on my feet. For a second, I thought my head had come off. Then, I had the strange sensation my neck was attached but was stretched beyond repair. My ears were ringing, pain shot down my arms and I felt a little queasy. I forgot, just for a second, where I was and what I was supposed to do. Jones looked me in the eyes, smiled knowingly, patted my helmet, and guided me back to my spot in line.

"Bell ringer!" I heard the coach yell.

I began my classes a few weeks later as an economics major. I had really wanted to study writing and literature but decided that economics would be a better way to make money. My first semester I took Economics 101, a macro economics class in a huge lecture hall; I also had a class called Statistics 13, an intro to statistics and the only class that taught me anything I would use as a trader; and a small advanced-placement Creative Writing class I had tested into.

I had never fully applied myself to my schoolwork in high school, always able to get by coasting and then cramming. I knew college would be more demanding and I was determined to be a more consistent student. The first college assignment I received was for my creative writing class: a two-page creative essay on the topic "The Place That Made Me." It was due in a week. I couldn't wait to get home and start writing -- I knew exactly what I wanted to write about.

The American River.

I skim-boarded, swam, rafted, and hung out there all my life. It was where I went to think. It was where I cleared my head. It was where I came from.

When I got back to my apartment, I dropped my backpack on the couch and started writing. By the time I looked back up, I'd written three pages about the American River and what it meant to me. I described a Friday night, the older kids driving their jalopies, with a keg or two wedged in back, to the parking lot near the river, where a couple of football players would carry the keg down to the shore. They'd usually charge everyone two dollars for all they could drink from a plastic cup. I wrote about cutting school on a sunny afternoon to sneak over the levy, down to the riverbank to see and hear and smell the water. I wrote about how the river was always changing, and yet it never changed. A constantly evolving touchstone.

I worked until the early morning to edit it down to two pages, rewrite a final copy, and then, when I was satisfied with my work, I typed it up neatly. Trouble was, I had completed the assignment a week before it was due.

I turned my paper in on the due date and had to wait a week to get it back from the teacher. It felt like a month. I was excited to see my grade, hopeful for an 'A' and some constructive feedback. Finally, the day the teacher had promised to return our papers arrived but I was so eager for my grade I could hardly pay attention to the lecture. When it was over, the teacher began calling names for students to raise their hands so she could return our papers. When she called my name, I noticed a change in her tone of voice and thought maybe she'd been impressed with my writing. I raised my hand and she put my paper face down on my desk without looking at me. I turned it over and looked for the grade and her corrections and comments, but the pages were unmarked except for a small note in red ink at the top of the first page.

"See me."

Nothing else. Not another mark on either page. My confidence plummeted. I was now sure my writing was so bad that she wanted to give me a second chance rather than an 'F' on my first assignment. Terrified that college was even harder than I feared, questioning if I belonged here and too embarrassed to talk to her in front of anyone else, I waited for the other students to leave. When they were all gone, I approached the teacher.

"Hi. Sorry. Umm," I stammered. "My paper just says *see me?*"

"Yes. Can I look at that again?" she asked.

I handed her the paper and she flipped back and forth between the two pages before looking up.

"Jalopy," she said. "Where did you learn that word?"

I told her the truth: I had read a *Hardy Boys Mystery* about a haunted jalopy when I was a kid and had loved sound of the word.

"These aren't contemporary words," she said, squinting at me through skeptical eyes. "Students don't use these words anymore."

I wasn't sure what the problem was but her criticism stung. Maybe I sounded too dated for college writing.

"I can replace them with more contemporary words if you want," I offered.

"I don't think I'm making myself clear," the teacher said. "I don't think you wrote this paper. I turned it over to the dean's office as a case of plagiarism."

The classroom wobbled for a second.

I felt queasy.

I couldn't believe what I'd just heard but when I looked into her eyes and I knew she was serious. She was looking at me like Perry Mason looked at a witness when he was about to prove the witness was guilty of the crime. I felt like someone had unexpectedly punched me in my stomach. I was dizzy and felt like I was about to throw up. I tried to breathe deeply and started to regain my senses. I wanted to yell at my teacher.

"It's my first college assignment *ever*," I wanted to shout, "and you think I cheated on it? Don't you think I would at least turn in one paper of my own just to see how I did before I started cheating? You think I came here to do nothing but cheat?"

But I just stood there, silent. Finally, she pointed to the door.

"The dean is expecting you in her office right now," she said, holding my essay out.

I took it from her and walked out without saying a word.

The English Department's office on the eighth floor of Sproul Hall, the tallest building in Davis. The students called it Sproul Sprawl because of the students often chose it as a means of suicide.

"I'm Rob Kovell," I said to the department secretary. "I am here to…I'm, umm…I was sent here by my teacher. To see the dean…"

 The receptionist looked down and shuffled some papers.

"Oh yes," she said. "I have you here on my list."

Not the Dean's list I wanted to be on, I thought to myself as I sat down in one of the uncomfortable university waiting room chairs to wait. What would I tell my parents about this? Or my football coaches? What would I say to my friends? Would they believe me? Or would they believe the teacher? I still couldn't breathe normally and my heart was racing.

 "You can go in and see the dean now," the dean's assistant announced.

I walked into the office and saw the dean sitting behind her desk. She was older, maybe in her sixties, and had short, faded blond hair and a motherly figure. She was regal looking and wore the exact clothes you would expect of a college dean.

"Have a seat, please," she said as I walked in. "I have a note here from Ms. Miller, your English teacher, as well as a copy of your paper. She thinks it is very good work. Too good. Ms. Miller is accusing you of plagiarism. Do you know the paper I am referring to?"

"Yes," I said. "It's the only paper I've written here."

"Can you tell me a little about how you wrote it?"

I launched into an explanation of the day I wrote the paper, how excited I had been, and how I'd worked late and finished it the night it was assigned. I told her about growing up in Sacramento, spending time on the American River near my home, and how I based my story on those experiences.

"Ms. Miller said I used outdated words like *jalopy*," I said. "But I thought we were supposed to. We were supposed to write a *creative essay*. This is the first thing I have done in college. I can't believe she thinks I cheated."

The dean listened and seemed sympathetic, but her expression darkened when she began to speak.

"These are very serious charges and we have a system in place to handle them," she explained. "If you fight the charges, you'll be brought up in front of an ASUCD Judicial Affairs committee for a hearing. The committee will either find you guilty or find a lack of evidence to proceed. If the committee finds you guilty of plagiarism, you will be expelled, not just from UC Davis, but all ten universities in the UC system. I have to inform you that if you choose to plead guilty before the hearing, you would only be suspended for the remainder of the first semester and then reinstated after the new year."

I sat there completely numb. The seriousness of my situation washed over me like the realization of being lost in the woods near sunset. I didn't know what to say.

"I wrote it," I said, but it sounded as unsure as I felt.

"You don't need to enter your plea until the hearing, which will be sometime in the next two weeks," the dean said. "Go to the student's Judicial Affairs Office in the student union, they will explain everything further and help you prepare for your hearing. Do you have any other questions for me?"

"No," I said. "Thank you."

I sat there for a moment more before slowly standing up and walking out of the office. I looked at the elevators but needed to keep moving so kept walking to the stairs at the end of the hall. I walked down eight floors to the ground level, pushed the door open, and stepped into a gorgeous, late summer day, a gentle breeze cooling my skin under the warm sun. The campus looked the same as it had an hour earlier -- full of life and possibility but I didn't feel a part of it anymore. I watched students rushing to class or the library – it felt strange that my world had virtually imploded and no one noticed.

I had no idea who to talk to. I wanted to talk to my dad but didn't know what I would say. The beginning of freshman year in college is a time when you are between friends – your high school friends scattered to their own colleges and your own college friendships are only days old. I didn't want the first thing people heard about me to be that I was accused of plagiarism. The Student Judicial Affairs office was all the way across campus but it seemed like the only place to go.

Walking across the quad I began to feel my strength coming back.

"I wrote it," I kept saying to myself. "I *wrote* it. *I wrote it.*"

By the time I reached the Judicial Affairs office, my fear had begun to abate, replaced by righteous indignation. I was ready to fight the charge and prove my innocence.

I explained my situation to the student working behind the desk. Marcia was a fifth-year senior with the look of someone who had already said a mental goodbye to their current place in life. I told her what had happened and that I was planning to fight the charges.

"Are you sure you want to do that?" she asked, with a clinical, dispassionate tone.

I was bewildered by her lack of sympathy.

"What?"

"This is a serious charge," she said. "Teachers don't make it lightly. The University will do everything in its power to prosecute you and if you lose, you will be expelled from the University of California system and have that on your record when you try to start somewhere else. Good luck with that."

"But I wrote it," I tried not to sound like a whining child.

"Maybe," she said, sounding unsure, "but if you can't prove it, you'll lose. This isn't a court of law, you're not assumed innocent. They'll ask you to write an essay in front of them, on a topic they choose, and give you thirty minutes and it better be as good as your paper."

"When will the hearing be?" I asked.

I was beginning to feel my confidence plummeting.

"We can schedule it right now," she said, as if it were a haircut I wanted. "How about a week from today? Next Thursday at 11:00 am?"

"Is that the soonest you have?" I asked, wanting this chapter to end.

"Yes. And you'll need a week to prepare your defense," she said. "You will get a grad student representative, who can help you but is not allowed to attend the hearing with you. Call this number during regular business hours and tell them what you need."

She handed me a pamphlet.

I left her office feeling devastated.

What if I lose? What if I choke writing whatever essay the panel surprised me with? Would they really expel me? If they did, it wouldn't matter that I was not guilty; every convicted man claims he's innocent. I would be a convicted cheater, a college flunk-out.

I wouldn't be able to face my dad. I wouldn't be able to face anyone. I began to wonder about confessing. I could take a 'red-shirt' year from football and not lose a year of eligibility and it would give me a few months to work full-time and save some money. I was living off-campus and would have to stay there and pay my share of the lease, but I knew I could get a construction job in Sacramento and commute. Hell, maybe I wouldn't even have to tell anybody.

But could I really confess to something I didn't do?

That would go against everything I had been taught. My mind was spinning out of control; one minute I was sure I would fight, the next minute I wanted to go back to the Judicial Affairs office and confess straightaway. I looked up from where I was standing and saw, across a practice field, the gym where the football coach's offices were. I remembered Coach Sochor telling the team that he was there for the players anytime, for anything. If we needed help. I started walking across the field towards the offices.

I went up to Coach Sochor's office, a place most players see only once, during recruiting trips. I told his secretary I needed to speak to the coach about an academic problem. She looked at me strangely.

"*Who* are you?"

"I'm a freshman offensive lineman," I said. "Coach told me if I ever had a problem on campus that I could talk to him."

"Ah," she said. "And what is your name?"

I told her my name and she disappeared into the inner office. Alone in the waiting area, I sat down in another uncomfortable university chair, identical to the one I had been in only an hour earlier at the English Department. As I did, I realized how crazy it was for a fourth string offensive lineman who never interacted with the coach at practice, hadn't even spoken to him except for once on a recruiting trip, to ask for a private meeting with the varsity Head Coach. As the minutes went by I imagined Coach Sochor perturbed, asking who the hell I was and telling the secretary to make up an excuse and get rid of me. I thought about getting up and leaving but remembered I had given my name.

The woman returned.

"Coach Sochor will see you now."

I sat down across the desk from him in an ancient steel chair, the kind that can only be found in a coach's office in an old gymnasium. The comfortable chair I had sat in on my recruiting visit was gone. Coach Sochor finished writing a note on a file, put the cap back on his pen, put the pen back in his drawer, and carefully closed the drawer. Then he placed the file neatly into his outbox. Finally, he looked up at me with all his attention.

"What can I help you with son?"

I took a deep breath, the first since I had talked to my english professor that morning. It felt good knowing I could unburden myself and my body relaxed, everything that had been spinning in my mind slowed. I began carefully recounting the day's events and tried to do it dispassionately.

Coach Sochor listened intently, looking me in the eyes the entire time. He was fully engaged. When I finished, his eyes turned upward, as if he were looking for a response on the ceiling. After a moment, he looked back into my eyes.

"Did you write the paper?" he asked.

The moment he spoke, I knew what I would do.

"I did," I said. "Thanks for your time."

 I called my dad that evening and told him the whole story.

"That's fucking ludicrous," Dad said, marking the second time ever I'd heard my father use that word. "Who the hell are these people? I've half a mind to call this *teacher* myself."

"Dad…," I tried to interrupt. I smiled at the way he said the word *teacher*, as if the word itself was contagious.

"Well, what the hell is she thinking?" he asked. But he didn't wait for my answer. "Don't worry, we'll do whatever it takes to win that hearing."

"Thanks Dad," I said. Unlike my coach, Dad never asked if I'd written the paper.

On the phone the next day, the grad student advisor assigned to my case told me to gather as much 'evidence' as I could before the hearing. Graded high school papers, letters from high school teachers and administrators - anything that would help prove I could write. Character references would help, especially from another university professor but that wasn't really an option for me, a freshman in his first weeks at a new school.

I found my worn copy of the Hardy Boys mystery, *The Tower Treasure,* in a box of books I had stored in my parents' garage. My uncle Bill had given me the entire Hardy Boys series for my tenth birthday. They were the first books I loved. In *The Tower Treasures*, a red-haired villain attempts to rob a ticket office, but when it goes awry, he steals a car and makes his getaway. The car belongs to Chet Morton, a friend of the Hardy brothers. Chet refers to his car throughout the book (as do the other characters) as his *yellow jalopy.* With some slick detective work, the Hardy Boys, of course, find the yellow jalopy and bust the robber.

I grabbed the whole box of books and left for my old high school to pick up two letters. Alice Kubo, the principle, had written a long letter praising my character, integrity, and academic ability. My senior AP English teacher, Mr. McRae, wrote that I had been "an outstanding writer" in his class the previous year. I thanked them both and, feeling somewhat ashamed even though I was innocent, I left as quickly as I could.

At home I added the things I had picked up to what I had already gathered. I had three A+ English papers from high school and copies of *The Rio Mirada*, the high school paper where I had served as both sports editor and writer.

The day of the hearing was the first real autumn day of the year. It was overcast and windy, leaves were falling from trees -- it felt foreboding. I arrived early but found the door to the hearing room was closed. I could hear people talking inside but didn't think I should knock. Fifteen minutes later I was invited in. I sat down in the empty seat facing the three people who would determine the course of my life. In violation of my sixth amendment right to confront my accuser, Ms. Miller was not there. On the table between the three judges were several stacks of books with titles like *River Landscapes*, and *Essays on Natural Landscapes*. I noticed some of them had multiple bookmarks in them.

The panelist in the middle started the hearing with a long outline of the proceeding and a description of the charge and the possible outcomes. Then he asked for my plea.

"I'm told you have denied the charge," he said. "I am now giving you one last opportunity to admit guilt and accept a suspension for the rest of this semester. This will be your last opportunity. Would you like to change your plea?"

"No, sir," I said.

"And you understand this is your last opportunity to do so?"

"Yes, sir."

He told me to present the material I had in support of my case and I handed everything across the table. I sat quietly as they looked through the paperwork I'd given them. I could see they were focusing on the papers I had written in high school. I saw one panelist raise an eyebrow to another after they both finished one of my papers. I couldn't tell if it was a good eyebrow-raise or a skeptical one. Once they had finished examining my documents, the judges asked me questions about the college essay and the places that inspired it. I gave long and detailed responses to every question, not stopping until one of them interrupted to thank me and ask another question. After a few of my detailed answers, the lead judge held up his hands for me to stop.

"I'm sure that's enough," he said. "Thank you. Do you have anything you would like to add?"

"I wrote the paper," I said. It was all I could think of. It was all that mattered.

"Thank you, Mr. Kovell," another judge said. "We need to deliberate alone. You can step outside and wait. We'll call you back in when we have a decision."

I felt calm as I left the room and sat down ready for a long wait. But, after only ten minutes, the door opened and I was invited back inside. My heart jumped as I tried to remember from watching courtroom TV dramas whether a quick verdict was good for the defendant or the prosecution. I couldn't remember. As I walked back into the room, I scanned their faces for clues but they were all stoic. I sat down and the head judge looked at me.

"This panel finds that there is not proof of plagiarism," he said. "The case is closed and there will be no further action."

I walked out into the windy autumn day. The campus was quiet, a few students hurrying into the library but otherwise the quad was barren. I had won my case but I felt defeated.

I didn't have my English class again until the following week. I arrived early in case Ms. Miller wanted to talk privately before class, but the classroom was empty. It filled with students, Ms. Miller was the last to arrive. She began the day's lesson immediately and did not finish until the hour ended. I went up to talk to her, not worried if anyone overheard me this time. She was holding the paper I had written. She was holding it out for me.

 I took it from her without looking at it and waited for her to say something.

 I looked down at the paper, it was still clean and unedited, except that the 'See me' had been crossed out and above it there was a small red 'B' next to it.

 At first, I didn't understand. I flipped back and forth between the pages to find more clues. There were none. She gave me a B on a paper she said was too good for me to have written. I looked up and saw she had a smug smile on her face. I could not imagine what she was thinking. There were so many things rushing into my head that I wanted to say but I couldn't figure out how to start. I took a deep breath but the words didn't come so I left without another word.

 I took the same path to the dean's office, burst in and said I needed to see the dean right away. This time I knew I wasn't on any list, but I must have looked serious because the secretary quickly disappeared into the dean's office. She came out and ushered me in.

 "The dean will see you now."

 Without sitting down, I placed the graded paper on the dean's desk. She looked at it and then asked me to sit down.

 "Let's get you into a different English class," she said.

Junior Year

I spent the summer before my junior year working for Red Devil Fireworks (*safe and sane!*) an outfit just like the place my Dad went to for our family's annual driveway pyrotechnics. From the day after school ended until a week before Independence Day, we worked twenty hours a day, seven days a week, assembling and putting up prefabricated stands in strip mall parking lots all over the Sacramento Valley. Although *stands crew* was a minimum wage job, we were paid more than double because we worked so much overtime.

By the end of June all the stands were up so there was nothing for us to do. The 40-hour work week cleaning up empty yards felt like a vacation. Then, a minute after midnight on July 5th, the chaotic dismantling began. We finished in early August, days before football camp opened. Working long hours had prevented me from spending money so I was started my third year of college in good financial condition.

My physical condition, on the other hand, was not as good as it needed to be going in to camp. My hopes that hard labor and the long hours I'd put in all summer would keep me fit enough for football were dashed. While my strength had improved from the summer of hard work, my cardiovascular fitness was way behind my teammates. I came into camp hoping to compete for a starting spot, or at least a role on special teams but by the first game of the season I had been relegated to the scout team offense. The *scout team* is a group of players who study the opponent's offense and run it against the starting defense to help them prepare for the game. Not in contention to play for their own team, scout players are actors playing the role of the other team.

I was disappointed to be put on the scout team as a junior but resolved to earn my way back to our own offensive group. Scout teamers are supposed to play hard, challenge the defense, and get beaten on most plays. This wouldn't get me back to where I wanted to be so I played every practice like it was game day which pissed off the starting defense and caused a chain reaction. The more I pissed off the starters, the harder they worked and the more the coaches loved it.

My lack of fitness combined with the relentless hitting re-aggravated a neck injury I'd had in high school and now in addition to a stiff neck I had shooting pain down my arms whenever I hit someone and a lingering numbness in my fingers after practice. I downplayed the symptoms to the team training staff because I was afraid they would pull me from practice. Toward the end of the season my neck got worse but I figured I could recover in the offseason. With only a couple of weeks left in the season everyone was hurting and I certainly didn't want to be the one that "wimped out."

At the Wednesday night full-contact practice before our next to last game, my neck was hurting worse than it ever had, but we had only two more full-contact practices left so I gritted my teeth and played through it. On a play near the end of practice, I pulled left from my guard position to lead an outside sweep. Heading up field and I saw that the linebacker I was to block was John Wright, a friend of mine – so, of course, I went at him as hard as I could. I don't remember the hit, only that I landed awkwardly and that when I tried to stand up, I couldn't. I was telling my arms to move underneath me, to push me up as they always do, but there was no response. The trainers surrounded me instantly and my teammates took a knee wherever they were. Their concerned faces and the silence on the field sent me into shock. I don't remember much until I was resting comfortably in the training room, able to control my arms again. The team doctor checked me further and kept me under observation for a couple hours, then sent me home to get some sleep and come back in the morning.

The next day I was fine, or at least no worse than before the hit. I went to see the team doctor who examined me thoroughly, checking the strength and sensitivity of all my limbs. When he finished, he told me that I had herniated a cervical disc and would be in pain for a few weeks. He went on to say that if I did the rehabilitation program he recommended, I would recover from the symptoms completely but the disc would always be more vulnerable to another injury.

"You're definitely not playing anymore this season," the doctor said. "And before I give you clearance to play next year, I'll need to examine you again when you report back to camp."

"Don't worry about that," I said. "I'm done with football."

I went to clear out my locker next morning when I knew the locker room would be empty. I took everything to the equipment manager who was sitting in the equipment room, as he always seemed to be.

"I'm done," I said, putting my gear on the table.

"For the year?" he asked without looking up. "Or forever?"

"Forever."

"Alright, in that case I have a checklist for you," he said. "Leave your shit there and follow me."

I followed him to a file cabinet in his office.

"This is a checklist from the university," he said. "Do everything on it, get the signatures you need and return it to me. Got it?"

I nodded.

"Good," he said. "Now follow me and I'll inventory your equipment and give you your first signature."

In addition to the equipment manager's signature I had to get my coaches and the team doctor to sign. I also had to meet with a graduate student nutritionist to discuss *health after football.* I silently groaned at the prospect of wasting time talking to a nutritionist but I set up the meeting hoping to make it short and get the signature as quickly as possible.

The graduate student must have sensed my impatience because she simply handed me a stack of *Healthy Eating!* and *Exercise!* printouts and said,

"I don't need to go through all these with you but you should look through them, for sure."

"Okay, thanks," I said, getting ready to leave.

"The only other thing I have to tell you," she added, "is that ninety-five percent of players who lose their football weight do it in the first two years. The longer you wait, the older you get, the harder it'll be."

I had spent the previous seven years bulking up, lifting weights, drinking protein shakes and eating all I could, trying to get above two hundred and fifty pounds for each season. Now I had to go the other way. I pictured the graduated ex-linemen who came to alumni events; they were either average-sizes and so fit you could hardly tell they had been big enough to play on the offensive line, or they were overweight and always seemed to have injuries. I knew which group I wanted to belong to.

From a financial standpoint, my football career ended just in time: I had burned through my savings and maxed out the student Visa card I got from a bank promotion I had happened by in the student union. It was a huge relief to turn my attention back to my finances without the time-consuming responsibility of football weighing on me. I felt like I could breeze though my final two years. At the time I was working three jobs, two of which were a half an hour away in Sacramento. I worked at a catering company setting up and serving at special events all over Sacramento and as a bellman at the Beverly Garland Motor Lodge near downtown. My third job was on campus working for the UC Davis Police Department as a *Cal Aggie Host*, providing student security at campus events. My favorite security assignments were, of course, the concerts -- artists like Elvis Costello and The Bangles passed through – and because of my size I was stationed either backstage or in the "pit" between the stage and the crowd. Concerts aside, most host duties were a lot less fun and usually involved standing around watching a door or gate, allowing entry only to those permitted. The worst host job was Bike Patrol. *Bike Patrollers* drove around campus in a big white UC Davis Police pickup truck, wearing greasy navy-blue coveralls with *Bike Patrol* stitched in giant gold letters on the back, impounding bikes that were illegally parked. The students generally referred to members of the bike patrol as "Bike Nazis" and weren't afraid to say so to our faces. Students on tight schedules, rushing to class, leaving their bikes in non-approved spots, would come out to find their bikes gone. Some panicked that their bikes were stolen and raced over to the campus police station only to learn their bikes were impounded and that they'd have to pay parking tickets and impound fees to get them back. It was such an unpopular job, if you were willing to do it, you could work anytime you wanted and as many hours as you could. I knew it wasn't a nice thing to do and felt bad for people whose bikes were taken, but somebody was going to do the job and I needed them money desperately.

Because it was so flexible and the station was near the center of campus, I could work even if I only had a few hours between classes. I would ride around in the UC Davis truck with bolt cable cutters to use on locked bikes (another costly surprise for students when they recovered their bikes). I'd expected some heckling when I got the job, but I was wholly unprepared for the vitriol that came from my schoolmates.

"You're just a bike thief asshole," said one.

"Fucking bike Nazi motherfucker!" said another.

The worst, however, were the pleas for mercy, not from the bike owners but from random students, usually female, witnessing the impounding.

"Hey, come on, someone really needs that bike," they would begin by cajoling me. "Can't you just leave a ticket?"

Or,

"You're stealing someone's bike, dude," they would say. "Come on, give someone a break. I can tell you're not a bad guy."

To which I would reply:

"I'm sorry but I can't. It's illegally parked and it's my job to impound it and I *really* need this job."

Somehow their sympathy would not extend to an overextended and broke fellow student.

"What a fucking dick you are," I was told. "You probably get your jollies on this little power trip. Go ahead be a Nazi, this little power is all you have! No girl would date a guy like you!"

I tried to minimize my bike patrol work by adding more shifts at my other jobs. Two shifts a week as a *Night Auditor* opened at the hotel where I was a bellman. I applied and was hired immediately. The Night Auditor works overnight from 11:00pm to 7:00am; does the bookkeeping and staffs the front desk. I loved the hours because they didn't interfere with any of my other jobs and the auditing work only took a couple hours so I could study for most of the shift. The first few shifts went well. I did get a lot of studying done and with the extra income I was able to stop working Bike Patrol, but by the third week exhaustion set in.

In the fourth week of auditing I was driving back to Davis after a night shift on a rainy morning. I lost focus for a what felt like a split second and in an instant the car was hydroplaning and began to spin out of control. At 60 miles per hour. On Interstate 80. I turned the wheel one way then the other, tried the brakes then gas pedal but nothing had any effect on the direction or the speed I was moving. After what felt like a long time, I felt the car slow as it slid off the pavement into the mud and grass of the shoulder, throwing mud up in the air and all over the car, completely blocking my sight. I was bracing for impact when the car came gently to a stop. It took a few seconds for me to believe it was really over and I was not only alive but unharmed. I listened to the raindrops on the roof of the car and gulped the air. Finally, I staggered out into the rain to assess the damage and saw that the car had stopped less than a foot from a tree.

I got back into the driver's seat, started the car and ran the windshield wipers so I could see. I put the car in reverse and backed slowly away from the tree. I stopped, put the car in drive, and drove slowly back onto the pavement, then pushed the accelerator hard to get up to freeway speed and merge back into traffic. I was moving at the speed limit a minute or two after spinning out of control. Life could change in one instant. At home I parked the car and inspected it more carefully, surprised to find no real damage, only mud caked everywhere.

"Nobody would even be able to tell I had an accident," I marveled at the thought.

When I walked into my apartment, my roommate Sean dropped the spatula into the eggs he was making and said,

"What the hell happened to you?"

"Lost control of my car on the freeway," I said, still shaky. "I spun around about ten times and almost hit a tree."

"Holy shit," said Sean. "How the hell did you lose control?"

"I don't know," I said.

"What do you mean you don't know?" Sean asked. "You were there, right?"

"Yeah," I said. "I guess I might have dozed off for a second."

"You fell asleep driving on the freeway in a downpour?" Sean said and shook his head. "That's a good way to die young."

He picked up the spatula to save his eggs.

Looking back, I am surprised it took Sean's reaction to make me realize I had to quit the graveyard shifts. I had been ready to hose down my car and get back to work, but when he put it into words – *you fell asleep at the wheel on the freeway in a rainstorm…that's a good way to die young* - I knew he was right. I quit the graveyard shift and went back to working Bike Patrol.

My catering work picked up over Christmas break and I got a few extra shifts as a bellman. All the jobs were in Sacramento so I stayed with my parents at their new condominium and slept on their couch. Whenever I had time off, I slept. I prided myself on the fact that I could fall asleep on that couch any time of day or night. But every time I woke up, whatever time it was, I found my dad sitting quietly in his chair, ready to talk with me, looking like he just sat down even though in some cases he'd been there for hours. We sat and talked – usually with a football or basketball game on TV in the

68

background, as we had throughout my childhood. I loved it. It was during one of these talks, a few days after seeing the movie *Trading Places*, that I asked Dad about a summer job on a trading floor. A few days later I would call Bill Grebitus so by the time I returned to UCDavis I had secured a summer job on the Pacific Stock Exchange.

*   *   *

I returned to school in January committed to doing better in school and beginning to lose my football weight. In order to have a good summer on the floor, I knew I had to have a good semester. I managed to organize all my classes on my Mondays, Wednesdays, and Fridays, which allowed me to work full daytime shifts at the hotel on Tuesdays and Thursdays in addition to my weekend shifts enabling me to permanently retire from Bike Patrol. Class days were long and difficult. I was on campus from 8:00 to 6:00, using the breaks between classes to keep up with my schoolwork. Tuesdays and Thursdays I worked 7:00 a.m. to 3:00 p.m. at the hotel and then whatever evening shifts I could pick up as a Host or caterer. But whatever the day's schedule, no matter what time I got home, I jogged around the suburban streets of Davis, so similar to the streets of my childhood, for an hour before bed. I also tried to eat healthier and smaller-sized portions. The nutritionist was right; with this minor effort I lost forty pounds before the summer started.

The remaining problem for the summer was a place to live. I looked through the San Francisco newspaper housing ads but there was nothing. The few places I could find available for short-term lease were out of my price range. San Francisco is not for the budget-conscious college student.

Then one afternoon I called my best friend from high school, Jon Underwood, at his fraternity house at the University of California in Berkeley. In high school, Jon and I had been nearly inseparable. We played football together, listened to music, and spent countless hours debating, or *arguing* as my mom called it (as in, *"Stop arguing!"*), music, sports, the weather, just about anything; we would take opposite positions and go at it for days. Our favorite debate was best band. Jon thought it was The Rolling Stones but I knew it was The Who. We quarreled about every detail of the two bands. For instance, on the topic of songwriting I would say:

"Behind Blue Eyes," as if this ended the argument.

"Moonlight Mile," he would reply with the title of his favorite Stones song.

"Baba O'Riley," I'd counter.

"Lovin' Cup," Jon would say.

"Magic Bus."

"Wild Horses."

The argument often continued to better guitar player (Townsend or Richards), better singer (Jagger or Daltrey), better drummer (Moon or Watts). The only concession I ever got from Jon was that Jon Entwistle was a better bass player than Bill Wyman. I would concede that, judged on *current* output, the Stones had an advantage -- The Who were never the same after Keith Moon's death and Mick and Keith seemed ageless, I'd admit. When we were in high school the Stones put out the wildly popular *Tattoo You* and before that *Some Girls*, while The Who managed *Face Dances* (decent but not their best) and *It's Hard* (to listen to, I'd joke to Jon).

But three years removed from high school, we weren't on the phone arguing about bands. Jon told me how school was going and about a few guys we knew from high school that were in his fraternity. I had called to tell him about my job on the PSE.

"What are you up to this summer?" I asked. "I might be living in the Bay Area."

"I'm living here in the SAE house and waiting tables at Henry's," he answered referring to a local restaurant. "What're you doing?"

"I got a summer job on the stock exchange in San Francisco," I said. "But I can't find anywhere to live."

"Live here!" he yelled excitedly. "It's going to be a few brothers and a bunch of girls from UC Santa Barbara staying here while they go to summer school. It's five hundred bucks for the whole summer and you can walk to BART and take a train into San Francisco."

"Everything about that sounds great," I said.

I couldn't believe my luck.

The next day I booked a room for the summer at the SAE house in Berkeley and everything was ready for my summer on the trading floor. I checked the train schedule for Bay Area Rapid Transit (BART) and found I could take the first train of the day from University Avenue in Berkeley to the Montgomery Street station in San Francisco, a short walk from the exchange.

At the end of the school year, I once again packed all my things into my Ford Escort to head to a new adventure. Although I didn't know it and had in fact signed a lease for an off-campus apartment the following school year, I was leaving Davis for good. On the last day of school, I drove west on Interstate 80 and took the University Avenue exit to Berkeley. I had visited Jon a number of times and knew my way to his fraternity house. It was Friday. I would be starting on the floor of the Pacific Stock Exchange the following Monday.

Berkeley

I arrived at the parking lot of the SAE house to a chaotic scene of people moving in, people moving out, people partying, drinking, laughing. There was a cacophony of sound: music was playing from at least three different sources, adding to the circus-like scene. It was a sunny June day after spring finals and before the summer term and the SAE house residents were clearly enjoying it. I parked in the unordered lot and left my keys in the ignition in case someone needed to move my car, as was the custom. I got out of the car and felt the sun reflecting off the white rocks in the parking lot, caught the scent of beer, and surveyed the chaos around me. Though it was similar to scenes playing out on the Davis campus I had just left, this felt different. I felt a distance from this party, this place and these people and I wondered if living here was a good decision.

It was not. The schedules of my housemates were almost exactly the opposite of mine. I woke up at 4:00 a.m. to shower and walk a mile to the BART station to catch the first train into San Francisco while they struggled to wake up in time for noon classes. The only people I saw in the house when I got up were *still* up, not already up. I showered one morning listening to one of the brothers violently throwing up while another drunkenly assured him he was fine.

Another time I inadvertently startled one of the female residents as she quietly left one of the male resident's rooms. She blushed and hurried down the hall, carrying a pair of high heels and her stockings. Often, around 2:30 in the morning, as everyone returned from the recently closed bars, a game of "kegball" would begin in the center courtyard. The rules of this game, as far as I could tell, were to take an empty beer keg, slam it violently around the cement courtyard, and make as much noise as possible. As I struggled to sleep the first night, listening to the opener of the kegball season, I sensed that my life had changed.

On Monday, I took my first BART train ride to San Francisco. I had never even been to the financial district where the Exchange was located. As I took the escalator up out of the train station and into the dark early morning city streets, I looked up in wonder at the tall buildings. I felt a rush of adrenaline surrounded by the other commuters moving hurriedly down the street.

Above ground, holding the directions to the exchange, I struggled to get my bearings on the strange city streets. Looking around for street signs, I saw people wearing the colorful smock jackets that I had seen floor traders wearing on television. I tucked the directions back in my pocket and followed the flow of jackets. At the entrance to the trading floor I gave my name and said I was there to see Marc Giacomelli at SWAT. Without a word to me, the receptionist picked up a microphone, squeezed a button, and made an overhead announcement,

"Marc Giacamelli to the front desk, Marc Giacamelli to the front desk."

Marc Giacamelli turned out to be a giant: nearly six feet, four inches tall and built like a refrigerator. He grunted something to me, quickly filled out some paperwork, peeled off a sticker that was a temporary employee pass, slapped it on my shirt and motioned for me to follow him. He walked back up the steps to the trading floor and hurried off in the direction he had come from. I followed him onto the floor like a boxer heading to the ring for his first fight. I had imagined this moment countless times over the past few months and my expectations were high. But even with dangerously high expectations, the energy and life of the trading floor blew my mind. Everyone moved like they had a mission, knew how to carry it out, and would not be deterred by anyone or anything. I wouldn't say it was confidence they all exuded as much as I would say it was competence. I loved it.

I followed Marc to the SWAT Trading booth on the edge of the trading floor. He threw me a green military camouflage patterned jacket and when I put it on, even though it was a little too small and ragged from overuse, I swelled with pride. With four pockets on the outside and four more on the inside, the jacket, I learned, served as your office and desk drawers. Marc brusquely introduced me to the SWAT team gathered in the booth, all somehow looking worn and tired but sharp and focused at the same time.

Marc was my boss and I would grow to respect him for his work ethic and integrity. That first morning he explained that SWAT executed stock orders on the NASDAQ market place which, at that time, was conducted mostly via telephone. The local options traders frequently traded stock in order to hedge the options they were constantly buying and selling in the pits, and we executed the trades for them. I started as a *runner*. Runners stand on the edge of the trading crowd and listen for stock orders. When the runner receives an order, he walks (running is actually illegal on the floor) back to the booth and repeats *exactly what he was told* to the phone clerk who executes the trade. Once the trade is finished, the clerk gives the details to the runner, who would then relay *exactly what he was told* to the client in the crowd.

Marc stressed that every detail had to be accurate every time. There were no small mistakes. He told me I would be shadowing a runner named Brian for the first week to learn the ropes. Brian was our runner in the Microsoft pit, where options on Microsoft and about thirty other companies traded. Pits were named after the most active stock but consisted of twenty-five to fifty, total. I remembered Bill told me that he traded in the Microsoft pit and I was thrilled at the prospect of seeing him.

At 6:25a.m., I followed Brian to the pit, about a hundred feet away from the SWAT booth, and we took our spot among the other runners and clerks lined up behind the traders.

At 6:30a.m., a bell rang to signify the market opening and suddenly the floor came to life. Game on. A couple of minutes later, a trader turned to Brian and said,

"Sell a thousand Softy at a half."

It made no sense to me but Brian turned, walked quickly back to the booth and repeated exactly what he had been told (easy enough), then he said,

"K19 FOC."

Uh oh, I thought.

Where did he get that last part?

When we were back at our station, Brian explained that every trader was given an acronym of a letter followed by two numbers, which was displayed on their badges they wore. That was where Brian got the *K19*. Then he told me that each market maker hired a clearing firm to clear their trades and the market makers wore their clearing firm's jacket. FOC was short for First Options Corporations and their coats were forest green. Brian reassured me that I would be able to memorize all the trader's acronyms and clearing firms in no time. He was right.

One thing about the order I hadn't needed to ask Brian; I figured out 'softy' was a nickname for Microsoft on my own. It was one of countless nicknames used on trading floors - IBM is *beamer*, The Standard & Poors S&P futures are the *spoo's*, and AT&T is simply *telephone*.

There is a large vocabulary of floor-speak and you have to figure out most of it for yourself or you'll be asking too many questions. A lot of the lingo is easy to figure out are obvious, but not all of it. The most difficult for me to learn was that the orders meant the fraction three-quarters and not multiple orders. So, if a trader wanted to sell Microsoft at one hundred and one and three-quarter dollars he would say,

"Sell me a grand at the orders."

The "hundred and one" is called the *handle* and is unspoken because we all know the market, and "the orders" means three-quarters. When I was first given an order like this, I stammered,

"What orders?"

All my question got me was an evil glare so I resorted to the rule of just repeating back exactly what was said to me. The language of the floor is crazy, colorful, and efficient and has a dose of dark humor.

After a week, Brian was promoted to phone clerk and I was working the Microsoft pit alone, handling our five to eight clients in the crowd. My first day on my own went fairly well and my anxiety faded with each successful order. Even when I did not understand exactly what I was told I would repeat it over and over to myself as I made my way back to our booth and then repeat it aloud to the desk. It sounds easy, but a wrong letter or number can lead to an error and a loss of money.

Then one day I received an order to sell stock, went to the desk and repeated it to Marc, who quickly executed it.

"Give him a fill at a half," he said. A "fill at a half" meant that he had sold the shares at the handle plus fifty cents. I went back to the trader.

"You're filled at a half," I said, holding out his copy of the trade ticket. I expected him to take it from me with the usual grunt of acceptance, but this time the trader turned to face me.

"Of course I am, you fucking idiot," he said. "It's bid three teenies better on the box."

What this meant and what I should do with the information was a mystery to me, as was what I had done to be called a fucking idiot. I stood there holding the fill paper out toward him until I realized he was not going to take it no matter how long I stood there. Not knowing what to do I went back to Marc and relayed the message, leaving out the part about me being an idiot.

"Tell him not to panic and hit bids and give me a not held order and I can get him a better price. But he'll fucking hold me if I miss it so I gotta bang bids."

I understood nothing and stood, mute, holding the fill paper between us. Finally, he ripped it out of my hand.

"Come on," he said. "Follow me."

I followed him out to the Microsoft crowd where he found our client.

"Look man, you always want your fill fast and you don't ever want to miss a level so I get it and hit the best bid," Marc told the client. "I can't do anything about what happens after that."

Marc put the paper firmly in the client's hand, leaving him no choice but to take it, and walked away. The client pocketed the paper and went back to making markets. Simple as that.

I loved everything about working on the trading floor. There was a method to the madness but also madness to the method. The only priority was getting the job done quickly efficiently and correctly every time. Whatever it took, however you looked; just get it done. For the first time in my life I felt useful.

The summer went by quickly and soon I understood how the floor worked. I learned how to tell the clerks like me from the members who were the only ones allowed to trade options in the pits. Then I learned how to tell which members were market makers and which were floor brokers. *Market makers* can trade anything and trade for their own account whereas *floor brokers* represent off-floor customers, who give them an order to trade a specific thing (or group of things) at a particular price. Sometimes the brokers are given leeway to try to get an improved price; these orders are called "not held" because if in the process of trying to get a better price, the broker gets a worse price, he is *not held* to the original market price. Floor brokers make a simple commission based on the number of contracts they execute. Market makers do not earn any commission. The only way a market maker can make money is to trade profitably in the market (buy low, sell high!) in excess of expenses. I only wanted to be a market maker.

Once I learned the players, I learned to keep up with the market and with all the stocks in my pit. This took complete focus and left me exhausted when my workday was done. The emotional intensity and intellectual challenge of the work were very tiring but it was also difficult physically. There were no chairs on the trading floor. All the participants had to stand in their spots from the moment before the market opened at 6:30am to just after the 1:00pm close. More than once I'd stumble up Bancroft Street after riding the BART train to Berkeley, with a trade ticket hanging out of my pocket, so intent was I on sleep and the next day at work. Unlike the exhaustion I felt in college, when I woke up the next day I felt reinvigorated and energetic, despite the early hour.

Working in the Microsoft crowd, I tried to stand as close to Bill as I could. I watched everything he did and tried to follow his logic. I began to see patterns in his trading which in turn helped me understand his basic strategy. In my second week, during the slow middle of the morning (lunchtime in NY), a broker brought an order into the crowd and asked where he could buy a large amount of October 50 Microsoft calls. Bill and the other traders offered a price where they would sell the options, which the broker relayed to his phone clerk. I remembered that the November 50 calls were offered in the exchanges electronic order book (or, "the book," as it was called), and knew that if the broker paid the crowd's offer for the October 50s, the November 50s would be a great hedge. I surreptitiously tapped Bill's arm and reminded him about the November calls. A few seconds later, the broker paid the crowd's offer for the October 50 calls.

"Sold!" Bill said to the broker. Then, "buy the book Nov 50's!" turning to the Order Book Official (OBO).

"Buy 'em with!" yelled most of the other traders.

When multiple traders compete for the same trade, the broker with the order determines who spoke first, second, third etc. He then offers the entire trade to the first respondent who has the right, according to exchange rules, to trade any part or all of the options. However, there is also an unwritten rulebook that governs behavior. The unwritten rule is that each trader takes no more than half of the remaining contracts, so a hundred would often be split 50 – 25 – 12 – 7 – 6. Bill bought exactly half the November 50s offered in the book, which I knew meant it was a great trade.

After he wrote up both trade tickets, Bill looked at me with a different light in his eyes.

"Good catch," he said.

The next morning Bill found me in the SWAT booth when he arrived around six and asked me to follow him to his booth near to the Microsoft pit. He started showing me his account statements from his clearing firm (FOC) and how he checked them against the previous day's trade tickets to make sure every detail had cleared correctly. If there was any difference between the two -- price, quantity, buy vs. sell, which option was traded, or if a trade appeared on one but not the other, Bill listed it on a sheet that said *Out Trades* at the top.

"It's pretty simple," Bill said. "Do you think you could handle this for me while you're here?"

"Yes!" I agreed, unable to conceal my excitement.

"Great," he said, smiling. "You can pick up my sheets at FOC and bring them down to the floor. Then make the out-trade list and leave everything for me here in my booth."

That day in the crowd Bill showed me the card that he marked after every trade in order to keep track of his activity. The cards were eight inches long and four inches wide and had columns and rows of lines printed on them and Bill showed me how he organized his card – calls on the left, puts on the right, front month options on top with the strikes written in the center column. Then he handed me a blank one.

"Why don't you keep one for me," he said. "Back me up."

I took the card and held it like it was an original copy of the Declaration of Independence. I neatly made an exact copy of the one I had watched Bill create. I kept that card updated with a religious fervor and never missed a single option. When my SWAT duties caused me to miss a trade Bill made, I would ferret out the information by asking the broker or finding the trade tickets before they were taken away so I wouldn't have to bother him.

From the start, I kept a more accurate card than Bill who, unlike me, had more important things to focus on every day. A few weeks later, Marc told me he was moving one of his best runners to join me in the Microsoft crowd.

"You don't have to do that," I protested. "I can handle it."

"I know you can," he replied. "So does Grebitus. That's why he wants you as his boy now."

With that I became a full-time assistant to a market maker. I joined Bill in the crowd and he wordlessly handed me a stack of call and put trade tickets, indicating he wanted me to write up *his* trades, too. I was thrilled to be able to focus completely on helping Bill, and willing to do anything for our cause. And I did, much of it not glamorous - fetching coffee and muffins, checking trade sheets, stocking his coat with trade tickets, picking up dry cleaning, and dealing with any and all things clerical. I tackled my tasks like my future depended on it and Bill gave me more and more responsibilities as the summer progressed.

July turned into August and I knew my internship was coming to an end. I lingered on the floor every day after work, wanting to soak up as much as I could before returning to my uninspired life as a college student. Living in the Bay Area had proven to be more expensive than I thought and I would be going back to Davis with very little savings. It felt like I was being sent back to prison after being exonerated and freed for a couple months. Still, if the thought of staying on the floor tried to enter my mind, I chased it away immediately, and focused on the goal of a college degree.

Then, eleven days before my final day on the floor, Bill asked me to come find him after the market closed. This wasn't unusual, Bill would often spend a few minutes at the end of the day sharing his strategy and explaining his activity that day. I loved these chats and finished my duties quickly. I found him at the periphery of the trading floor.

"You seem to like it down here," Bill said.

"Yeah, I love it," I said smiling. "Thanks for making this happen for me. I don't want it to end."

"Well, that's why I wanted to talk to you," Bill said. "You're scheduled to leave us in a few weeks, right?"

"Two more weeks," I said.

"Well, I wanted to see if you would to stay a little bit longer than that." Bill said.

It was so unexpected that it took me a few seconds to realize what he was offering me.

"If you do stay," he continued, "I'll back you as a market maker. You can clerk for me for a couple more months and then you'll start trading."

I couldn't process what he said. I stood there silently. I had not once even dreamed that this would be anything other than a summer job - my wildest dream had been to return to the floor after graduation. Although every ounce of me wanted to stay, I quickly said:

"Oh, thank you, but I can't do it now," I replied. "I've got to finish college. I would love to come back after graduation, though, if the offer is still good."

The words sounded like someone else was speaking them.

"Okay," Bill said. "You know how it is down here, I can't make any promises about next year. But look me up when you finish with school and we'll see."

I thanked him again and headed home. On BART that afternoon, as the train travelled deep under the San Francisco Bay, my spirits soared. Not because I thought I could accept the offer, but just because I had received it. I had chosen this path, sought it out, and I felt like I had succeeded. Although I was only a summer intern, I was a great one. I turned my mind to my upcoming school year and felt my spirits crash. I would need to carry eighteen units of courses each semester in order to graduate – and that would be in addition to working a couple of jobs. It wasn't like I was wrestling with the decision, there was no decision to make; I was sure of what I had to do and was going to do it.

Still, over the next week I let myself imagine what it would be like if I stayed; what it would be like to be a member, to try my skills in the options market with no other obligations to distract me. I pictured myself in a forest green FOC market maker jacket, member badge clipped to the lapel, standing in the crowd, trading with a broker and giving a stock order to the SWAT runner to hedge my trade. I felt elated just imagining myself as an options trader. But I also loved picturing Demi Moore falling in love with me -- I knew neither was going to happen.

Thursday afternoon I had to move into Jon Underwood's room for my final week because the brother who had rented my room for the fall semester arrived. Jon helped me move my things across the courtyard to his room. When we finished moving my stuff, we went out for dinner at a local pizza place. We drank beer and played foosball until eleven at night – *way* past my bedtime, but when I finally got to bed I couldn't sleep. I stared at the ceiling listening to Jon's breathing turn to sleep as my thoughts raced in unconnected circles. I decided to match Jon's sleep breathing – taking deep slow breaths in rhythm with my roommate. My mind calmed down and I began to feel relaxed. Still not the least bit sleepy, I took as deep a breath as I could and let it out slowly. When I finished exhaling I knew I had to stay on the trading floor. I would drop out of college and accept Bill's offer. I hadn't reasoned my way to this decision, hadn't listed pros and cons on separate sides of a paper, didn't weigh the alternatives - I just suddenly *knew* I had to do it.

I felt so clear and peaceful about my decision but I had to say it out loud to make sure it was real.

"Hey Jon, you awake?" I said.

"No," Jon replied.

"I'm going to quit college and become an options trader," I said, trying it out.

I heard Jon turn over in his bed.

"Great," he said. "Go to sleep."

The next morning at work I was desperate to talk to Bill but knew there wouldn't be an opportunity until after the market closed. I told him during a slow moment that I wanted to talk to him after the close. He agreed.

Hours later I hurried through my closing duties and found Bill in his booth.

"Hey kid," he said. "What's up?"

"Would you still be willing to back me if I stay?" I asked, getting right to the point.

"Absolutely," he replied.

"Well, I'd really like to accept," I said. "But I want to talk to my dad first."

"Is he going to object?" Bill asked.

"I don't know," I said. "He's always insisted I get a college degree, but I really want to do this now and I think I can make him understand."

I looked down at the litter-strewn floor.

"And even if he doesn't," I continued, "I think I'll stay. I just want to talk to him first."

"I guess we'll see," Bill said.

That afternoon, I took the BART train to the Ashby Avenue station in Berkeley where I had parked my car that morning and began the ninety-mile drive to my parent's house in Sacramento. There was the usual bad Friday traffic and the drive felt like it would never end. I rehearsed my speech a hundred times in ninety miles but it never sounded quite right. I didn't want to say, "I'm doing this no matter what and I don't care what you think," but I also didn't want to sound ambivalent.

Three hours later I arrived at my parent's house ready to justify dropping out of college after three years to be an independent options trader with no guaranteed income. I was ready for a fight and prepared to stand my ground. Walking from my car to their front door I breathed as deeply as I could and stretched my body. With my hand on the doorknob, I paused. The point of no return. I took one more deep breath, turned the doorknob and walked into the house.

It felt empty. Both the family room and the living room were quiet and dark.

"Hello?" I called out, hoping to find my parents together. It would be Dad's decision but I knew Mom would lend moral support and keep the conversation from getting contentious. My dad answered me from the kitchen.

"I'm in here," he called out. "Come on in and join me. There's something I want to talk to you about."

I walked into the kitchen and found him at the breakfast table giving himself an insulin shot in his thigh. The family dog, a mutt named 'Sassy,' was lying at his feet as she did every time he injected himself and, unwilling to abandon her post, greeted me with only a wag of her tail. I stood and waited for him to say whatever it was he had to say.

"Bill Grebitus called this afternoon," Dad said as he pulled the needle out of his leg. "He told me he offered you a trading position on the floor. He also told me that you wanted to accept it."

I was dumbfounded and couldn't respond. Finally, after a couple of breaths, words flooded into my head. This was unfair! I needed to be the one to tell him so I could explain. But before I could speak, Dad continued,

"Robert, I am very proud of you for making this decision," he said. Adding, simply, "good luck."

San Francisco

The following week was a scramble. Jon's roommate was moving in Saturday so I needed to find another place to live by then. But before signing a lease in San Francisco I had to get out of the one I had signed for the school year in Davis. Luckily, there is always a shortage of housing in college towns so, with just a couple phone calls I was able to find someone to take over my lease. Now officially homeless in a week, I scanned the litter-strewn trading floor for the classified section of the San Francisco Chronicle. I found one and took it back to the SWAT booth. I found the 'apartments for rent' and began to scan the column. The listings were ordered from cheapest to most expensive. Unfortunately, only the first two listings were within my price range. I called both numbers and set up visits the following day.

My first visit was at the cheapest apartment listed in the newspaper. I arrived at the address and found myself in front of an adult video store. I checked to verify I had the right address. Looking back up I noticed there was a locked glass door adjacent to the store's entrance with the telltale multi-button unit buzzer. I peered inside and saw a ransacked lobby with mailboxes, a torn sofa, and a broken table covered with abandoned mail. Opposite the door there was a dimly lit, narrow stairway leading up above the store. I didn't go in.

I drove to the other address on my list and decided to do a drive-by before parking the car. I was encouraged. The building was a very ordinary, five-stories high and occupying about a quarter of the block on a busy one-way street a few blocks from City Hall. Across the street was the Motel Capri - clearly not a five-star destination - but there were no adult video stores in sight so I barely looked at the motel. It wasn't optimal but it was my only choice.

I parked around the corner, walked back to the building, and rang the buzzer for apartment 1A where the building manager lived. After a long pause, a loud and distorted voice crackled through the speaker but I didn't understand a single word. When the talking stopped a loud buzzer sounded so I pushed the door open and walked into the lobby to look around. It wasn't fancy, but it was clean and the furniture undamaged. There was a table in the center with a fake plant on it, an elevator to the left, stairs straight ahead, and one door on my right. On the door was 1A. I knocked.

"Come on in, its unlocked," I heard from inside.

I opened the door and walked into a narrow hall. The rest of the apartment, and whoever was in it, was behind a curtain of crazily colored bead strands, like you might have found in a massage parlor in 1975.

"Hello?"

"Come on back!" called a woman's voice from behind the curtain.

I pushed through the beads into a smoky studio that smelled like a mixture of patchouli, incense, and marijuana.

"You're here to look at the studio on five, right?" She asked.

"Yeah, I called yesterday."

Without asking for my name or any other information, she led me up the elevator to a door near the middle of the fifth floor. On the short trip, she described each of her three ex-husbands, told me most of her life story, and that she suffered from depression. I struggled to think of something to say before realizing she didn't want or expect a response. At the door, she continued a story about her second ex-husband's drug problems while she struggled to find the right key to open the lock. After trying every key on her large key ring, she started over and the first one she had rejected worked on its second try. We walked into a small but well-lit studio apartment, a large closet on the right near the door, a small bathroom to the left, and a very small kitchen at the far end. The entire apartment wasn't much bigger than my room in the SAE house across the bay, but it cost more per month than that room had for the entire summer. It was within my budget, though, and it was clean and seemed safe so the first thing I said to her was,

"Can I move in this weekend?"

Enlisting the help of Tim Reilly, a friend from high school, I loaded my few possessions, mostly clothes and books, into his pickup truck. On the way from Berkeley to San Francisco we stopped at an inexpensive furniture store in Oakland to buy a bed and dresser. Even though we had found a discount furniture outlet, I realized I didn't have enough money to buy a dresser, bed frame and mattress. Making the obvious choice, I had Tim help me load the mattress and dresser into his truck. We drove across the Bay Bridge to San Francisco and my new home. We wrestled the mattress up five flights of stairs (the elevator being too small) and then into my apartment. One more trip for the dresser and then maybe two more for clothes and boxes and we were done. Tim had to get back to Sacramento and left as soon as we finished.

"Thanks, man," I said. "I really appreciate it."

"No problem," he said. "Good luck with everything!"

I locked the door behind him and turned to look at my new home. It wasn't much but I felt like I was living in the penthouse of the Ritz Carlton.

The following Monday I woke up before my 4:00am alarm sounded and took my time getting ready. I was able to leave a half hour later than I had from Berkeley and still arrive on the floor at the same time. Stepping out of my building onto Franklin Street at 4:30 in the morning, I noticed a couple of women across the street outside the Motel Capri. As I walked to my car one of them yelled,

"Hey Baby, you looking for a date? Come on over here, I got a half hour left on my room."

I hurried to my car without even turning my head. Driving in that morning I felt different: full of purpose, alive. I parked under the Bay Bridge, in one of the few free spaces near the financial district (there were some advantages to the early hours) and walked the half-mile to the exchange. I knew I was passing through a door and that the door would be forever locked behind me and I was exhilarated.

The final turning of that lock came that very Monday when I called UC Davis to officially drop out. I used the SWAT phone to call the UC Davis Registrar's office and left a message:

"Hi, this is Robert Kovell, K-O-V-E-L-L. I am registered as a fourth year for the fall semester but I will not be returning to school. Thank you."

With that, I became a college dropout.

I was scheduled to start as a trader within a few months so I sought out anything I could to learn more about options. The trouble was, there weren't a lot of books about options at that time and none that explained the strategies a market maker used. It was like an ancient art that could only be learned from those who practiced it. The only relevant book I could find was written by an economist, Lawrence McMillan, and titled *Options as a Strategic Investment*. Every market maker had the book, but none had read it. I borrowed Bill's unopened copy.

It was four hundred and eighty-two pages of dry text, mathematical formulae, and charts and graphs of every kind. Published by the New York Institute of Finance, it was intended more for academics than floor traders, and reminded me of my college textbooks. Although I read it every evening, I got as little out of it as I had the textbooks. Everything I knew about my new job, I had learned from Bill or figured out myself while working on the trading floor, but this gave me a great practical understanding of my challenge.

A market maker is required to maintain a fair and orderly market at all times by providing a continual bid (a price where he will buy) and offer (a price where he will sell) for every option in his pit. As a result, a market maker cannot control whether he buys or sells an option; he can only control the price of the trade. Markets are made around what the crowd considers the *fair value* of the option, so that whichever side the trade it will be at an advantageous price. We called this difference between fair value and trade price *edge*. Anybody can stand in a crowd and respond to brokers and make trades with *edge*, but only the good ones can turn it into profit. The fair value of the option is based on the current price of the stock, so when the stock moves the option moves with it, which means a market maker needs to make an offsetting trade before the stock price changes or risk losing the edge. It is this second trade, or *hedge,* that separates successful traders from bankrupt ex-traders. There were no books on this kind of trading; McMillan assumed the reader cared about the strategy of a position, not the price. I was fortunate to learn the art of *hedging* from an experienced floor trader. If I hadn't had Bill as a mentor, I would never have learned it and my career may have been very short.

The only resource that applied directly to being an options market maker was a set of VHS video tapes that my clearing firm, First Options, offered to new clients. The tapes contained a series of lectures given by an ex-market maker named Marty O'Connor. Marty had been a good trader and understood risk well, but his presentation style was desert dry and the video lacked any production - the camera never moved, obviously on a tripod without an operator. Marty was standing in the center of the picture, behind a lectern, in front of a white background, reading his notes while he spoke. No graphs, charts, or graphics of any kind. Just Marty describing in monotone what happens in an options pit. Until then I hadn't thought it would be possible to make an options pit sound like an accounting office.

The videos were proprietary and could not be checked out. They were only available to be viewed in First Options' offices during business hours. So, after getting up at four in the morning, rushing to the exchange, working on the floor until two or three o'clock in the afternoon, I would go upstairs to sit alone in a small office to watch the lectures. Despite always bringing a large coffee with me, I never made it through an entire lecture without falling asleep.

For me though, the real classroom was the trading crowd I was standing in every day. I was never a good book (or video) learner, whether I was learning to golf or to swim, to drive a truck or trade options. I learned from observation and practice, not explanation or theory. The best way to learn how to swim is to jump in the water. Clerking for Bill gave me a front row seat to watch an excellent market maker do his business: I watched how Bill priced options, hedged trades, managed risk. I took in everything he did. I even had the same thing for breakfast: a bran muffin and a latte. Maybe I learned something from staring at McMillan's book at night or trying to fight sleep through Marty's videos, but I learned the *important* things from Bill. Not that he explained everything to me, though occasionally he would pause to point something out or to use a sports analogy. Rather, Bill would go about his business knowing I was studying his every move.

I loved it and soaked in as much knowledge as I could. I took home Bill's recap sheets every day and reviewed every trade he had made. On the weekends, I charted (by hand, in legal notebooks) Bill's positions and his trading activity, the hourly price changes of every option, and the resultant profit or loss. I didn't fail to notice there was a lot more profit than loss. What took me most of the weekend to create and analyze could be done in seconds today with a simple spreadsheet program and a cheap laptop.

A few weeks later Bill asked me to join him for breakfast at *Muffins Muffins,* the bakery in our building's lobby. This was unprecedented, Bill rarely took a break during market hours and when he did, I always stayed behind to watch his positions and would run to get him if anything significant happened. We left the pit after the morning rush, when it is lunchtime in New York, and went down to the bakery. When we sat down with our muffins and lattes, we talked briefly about the 49ers comeback win over the Bengals the previous day before getting down to business.

"Alright," Bill finally said. "You ready to be a market maker?"

"I am," I replied.

"Excellent," Bill said. "I filed papers with the exchange and the clearing firm yesterday and it looks like you'll start November first."

Bill went on to explain how our deal would work but I couldn't focus on what he was saying because I kept hearing *you start November first* in my head. Five more weeks and I would be a market maker. Bill finished explaining the deal and I understood the basics. We would set up a limited partnership, which Bill would fund with thirty thousand dollars (an impossibly huge amount of money to me at that time,) and I would be responsible for all of the trading decisions. Profits would be divided equally until Bill received $180,000. That's a five hundred percent return on his original investment, which sounds usurious, but is actually fair; new market makers fail (and lose the thirty thousand dollars) much more often than they succeed, so there has to be a high return from the winners to offset the losers.

I spent a couple of weeks signing membership papers, opening an account at FOC, and creating our limited partnership. Bill had his accountant, Don Mankin, draw up the LP documents and I took a rare break from the trading day to meet with him and finalize the partnership.

"I've fill out most of the paperwork," Mankin began, "I just need to know what you want to name the LP."

I hadn't even thought about naming the business.

"I have no idea," I said. "What do most people name them?"

"Oh, I've seen them named just about anything," he replied. "Some folks use their name combined with the word 'trading' or 'investments', some go with a Greek God or some other crazy sounding thing. Whatever you want."

I had a thought.

"Can I call it BTR Trading?" I asked.

"I'll have to check with the state to see if it's taken," he said. "If not, you've got it."

"Great, thanks," I said.

"You probably won't tell me, but I'm going to ask anyway: what's BTR stand for?"

"You're right," I said, smiling. "I'd rather not say."

"Yeah, you're a trader," he said with a shrug. "Superstitious and secretive."

Hearing *you're a trader* gave me a rush of dopamine and I was glad I kept the real name to myself. The big secret I was keeping: BTR meant *Born to Run*. I named my first trading partnership after a Bruce Springsteen song about getting out and making a new life.

The Crash

Throughout my first summer on the floor, the *great bull market* that started in 1983 continued its march upward. On August 25th, my second day in my new apartment, the Dow Jones Industrial Average closed 2,722, a new record, a forty-four percent increase in just twelve months. Microsoft, despite many vocal critics who said software companies would never make a lot of money because of piracy and competition, had done even better -- quadrupling in the same period.

In September the market averages slid from their record levels, but nobody seemed worried. It was a healthy pull-back after a long run. Microsoft also stopped going up, but despite its recent outperformance, didn't drop as much as the market. Then, on September 21st, Microsoft split its stock 2:1, which means each shareholder receives the same amount of stock they currently own, doubling their position. Companies split their stocks for corporate governance reasons and it should have no effect on the value of the company – each share is doubled but the stock price is halved, so instead of owning one hundred shares of a fifty-dollar stock, the shareholders own two hundred shares of a twenty-five-dollar stock. It's like changing a hundred-dollar bill for two fifties. However, for whatever reason, stocks often do rally after a split, and Microsoft took this to an extreme; going from fifty-three to seventy-nine, a sixty-seven percent increase, in the first eleven trading days after the split. Spirits were high in the pit; traders busy and prospering from the activity and movement. I heard more than one market maker repeat a market axiom I would remember for my entire career.

"The trend is your friend."

On Wednesday, October 14th, two days before the October options expired, the Dow Jones Industrial Average fell ninety-five points, the most ever in a single day. Still, the feeling on the floor was bullish and everyone remained buoyant. In fact, traders were rooting for the market to fall further at the end of the day and make it first ever one hundred-point daily move. Microsoft held up pretty well, dropping two dollars to seventy-one. The next day the market was up a little, but not a very strong rebound after the big drop. The floor was eerily quiet, especially since there were a record number of options expiring the next day.

Friday morning there was bad news from the Middle East. Iran had hit two American flagged vessels with missiles, raising tensions in the oil-rich region. This kind of news would usually have little effect on the market, but on this particular day it was the excuse the market needed to resume its fall.

And fall it did.

The floor was the busiest I had seen it and I worked my tail off to keep Bill caught up with the volume and the movement. Large moves in stocks near options expiration are very risky for options traders.

Microsoft opened unchanged that day, around seventy-one, and despite the down market, immediately resumed its upward run, reaching 74.50 by the end of the first hour of trading. The October 75 calls, expiring that day, went from a nickel to over a dollar in the same period - a two thousand percent increase. Then around midday, Microsoft couldn't continue to buck the market's trend and fell back to seventy-one as quickly as it had risen. The October 75 calls were worthless again, but now the October 70 puts were exploding. With all the volatility and activity, I had a hard time keeping track of Bill's position but I could tell he was doing well.

During the last hour of trading the selloff in the market intensified. There was a brief cheer as the Dow Jones finally ticked down a hundred points, but it didn't last long because of the heavy activity – the day's volume *doubled* the exchange's previous record. The selloff continued in the final hour and Microsoft fell through seventy like a knife through butter and went straight to sixty-five. The October 70 puts went from ten cents to five dollars in less than an hour. The market fell until the closing bell mercifully rang. When I finished my work for the day, I bought a sandwich from the deli across the street from the exchange, went home, ate and went straight to bed. I was asleep before seven o'clock.

I woke up early Saturday and began my recap of Bill's week of trading. Because of the high volume, it took me twice as long as it usually did. When I finished I saw that my instinct had been correct: Bill had made a month's worth of profit on Friday alone. I also saw that he had ended up with a lot of downside risk going into Monday. It's difficult to control what your position will be after expiration and Bill was longer than he wanted to be. I knew he would sell stock as soon as the market opened to close the risk and lock in his profits from Friday, but where would the stock open?

When the market opened down more than two hundred points on Monday, there was no cheer. Bill's expression didn't change, but I knew he was hemorrhaging money. After the opening he handed me a piece of paper.

"Give these to Marc," he said.

As I hurried to the SWAT booth I looked at the paper, there were market orders to sell stock in Microsoft and five other NASDAQ stocks Bill traded. A *market* order has no limit, you sell the shares immediately in the market at any price. Typically, a market order is filled in seconds, so when thirty minutes passed and I hadn't heard anything from Marc I went back to the booth.

"What's going on with Grebitus' orders?" I asked. "We should be done by now."

"Nobody's buying anything," was all Marc said.

I relayed that back to Bill who shook his head.

"Screw it," he said. "Just cancel them."

I cancelled the orders and started to pray the market would rally. Near the end of the session, Bill handed me another piece of paper with the same stock orders on them except one – Microsoft, his biggest position.

"Go work those yourself," he said wanting me to go to the booth and call the dealers myself.

"No Microsoft?" I asked.

"No," Bill said turning back to the pit.

"Grebitus gave me the market orders back, who should I call?" I asked Marc when I got to the SWAT booth.

"Call anybody you fucking want to," Marc said. "Nobody's answered a phone in hours." He held out the two phones that were resting on his shoulders near his ears and I could hear the droning rings.

"What about Mayer Shweitzer?" I asked. "We have a direct line, they've gotta answer."

"Vogel picked up a half hour ago to tell us to stop calling, they weren't buying anything," Marc replied. "He sounded like shit."

I picked up two phones and called Merrill Lynch on one, Goldman Sachs on the other. No answer. I tried Morgan Stanley and Bank of America but still got no answer, just a sea of ringing phones. I kept trying for the final hour of trading but nobody answered. I failed to fill one market order. When I told Bill a 'nothing done' on all five markets he just shrugged. On any other day he would have fired me for incompetence.

Bill and I went through his positions after the close and it was obvious he had lost a ton of money. Maybe everything. Plus, because of my inability to sell the stocks, he had a lot of downside risk and if the market continued falling he would end up with a big deficit. We sat in silence as this sunk in.

"Let's get out of here," Bill said. "I need to go home and talk to my wife."

This was *Black Monday*, the great stock market crash of 1987. It remains the biggest single day drop in the history of the American stock market. What I remember most about the floor that day was the quiet. Even though we set another volume record, the floor felt more like a funeral home than a stock exchange. The further the market fell, the quieter it became. Some traders were making a fortune, others were losing everything but they all wore the same shell-shocked expression. The crash was unprecedented and nobody knew what would happen to the economy, although plenty were stocked up on ammunition and dried food.

Stepping out of the building into a bright Indian summer day in San Francisco, I was surprised to see people walking along, going about their business as though nothing had happened. (This was 1987 and information traveled at what we would now consider a glacial pace, so most of them probably *didn't* know what had happened.) I don't know what I was expecting to find on the street, but I expected *something*. Maybe not people rioting or jumping off buildings, but something. Many people on the sidewalk had lost a lot of money that day but they were going about their business. I didn't have any money to lose in the market, I had just lost my dream, and I wanted to go about my business too – I just wasn't sure what it was going to be.

I walked out of the financial district up to the Bay Bridge where my car was parked, but when I got there I continued down to the waterfront and sat down. I sat there for an hour and emptied everything from my mind, focusing on the feeling of the sun on my skin, the smell of the water, and the distant sound of cars crossing the bridge above me. Finally, as the sun began to set, I went to my car and headed home. I knew I didn't have any food for dinner but was too tired to stop anywhere. I fell into bed exhausted but wired at six-thirty that night. Lying there awake, I tried to look into my future, but for the first time in my life I couldn't see anything there. I knew I had to keep going as long as Bill needed me. I told myself I could worry about my future later. There would be a ton of work to do over the next weeks and even knowing Bill might not be able to pay me, I was happy to have something to do.

I slept soundly for a few hours but woke up at three o'clock in the morning with my mind already spinning at top speed. I knew right away I wouldn't get back to sleep so I got up, started the shower, and brushed my teeth. Going through my morning ritual with the ease of routine allowed me to slow my thoughts, and by the time I was clean and dressed for it felt like a normal workday. Unfortunately, I was ready for work an hour early and had nothing to do. Suddenly, my apartment felt tiny and drab and depressing. With nothing left to busy myself with my anxiety began to get the best of me so I grabbed my keys and hurried out the door. Driving to work, I wondered how early the office opened and if I would be the first one there.

Walking up Pine Street twenty minutes later, I saw that the FOC offices (which contained our office) were alive with light from every window. I quickened my pace. As

I did every morning, I went directly to our mailbox in the FOC administrative office to pick up Bill's "sheets." These included a *Trade Confirmation Report* (which I needed in order to clear our trades from the previous day), an *Equity Report* (to find out if I had a future on the floor), and the *Position Summary* (which I didn't need but usually delivered to Bill).

I hurried from the elevator to our mailbox at FOC but it was empty.

"Hey Joe, where's our stuff?" I asked the FOC clerk.

"Grebitus picked it up a half hour ago," he said without looking up from his work.

Bill had never arrived before me, and I was an hour early, but these were extraordinary days. I walked into our office and found him looking a little tired, staring at the reports in his lap. Maybe it wasn't as bad as I'd feared. He tossed the reports onto my desk.

"Get to work," was all he said.

I sat down and oriented the sheets so I could to read them. Just as they would every morning of my trading career, my eyes immediately found the *Net Liquidating Balance* (*net liq*) which represents the total value of your account on the previous day's closing prices. It was your bottom line, your account balance, your total capital; the only number that *really* mattered. I immediately noticed Bill's net liq was a big number like it always was, however it was different than other days because it had parentheses around it. I had been around long enough to know this meant it was negative – Bill had lost all his money and owed this amount to the clearing firm.

My head jerked up and I saw Bill had been waiting for my reaction. He met my eyes, shrugged, smiled and said:

"See you on the floor."

On *Black Monday* six hundred and four million shares traded on the New York Stock Exchange (NYSE). Although this is a fraction of an hour's worth of volume today, in 1987 it was a record. By a long shot. The average daily volume was just over one hundred-fifty million shares, and the busiest days rarely exceeded two hundred million. Friday, the day before the crash, 334 million shares traded, the first-time volume exceeded three hundred million. With all this volume, came a great deal of *out trades;* trades where the counterparty doesn't "know" the same details as you do or doesn't "know" the trade at all. Out trades happen every day and are considered a cost of doing business in such a chaotic environment, but with the large ranges of stocks on Black Monday, even small out trades became big. Usually when you had an error overnight, the stock would be within a dollar or two of price where you traded. So, a one thousand-share error could cost you between one and two thousand dollars. That Monday some stocks had a range of fifty dollars so the same one thousand-share error would cost you fifty thousand dollars. And the volume created a record number of out trades, all of which needed to be negotiated.

Before electronic trading and clearing, a good out trade clerk was worth a fortune. Most times out trades never become errors because you were able find the other participant in the trade and agree on the details. However, if the guy you are looking for has a fifty thousand dollar winner on his hands, he might make himself hard to find. Of course, if he has a losing out trade, he will find you immediately.

There was so much work to do that the exchanges decided to close early every day for the rest of the week to allow the out trade clerks to catch up. I worked long hours that week to insure Bill received all the trades he was due, and by the end of the week our error account was slightly higher than it had been before the crash. I had done my job well.

When the market was open that week it rallied back from its lows. This news was good news for Bill's market making account - the stocks I had been unable to sell rallied significantly and my failure *saved* Bill tens of thousands of dollars. By Wednesday the account was back to zero and by Friday it was positive. The market felt more stable every day, but still no one felt safe. Bill didn't say a word about my future and, afraid of the answer, I didn't ask.

The following week the account balance continued to climb until it was nearly back to its pre-crash level. Still, it felt tenuous. Every day, newspapers and television news quoted financial experts on the similarities to the crash of 1929, which was the catalyst for the Great Depression. Even before the crash there were many economic doomsayers on the trading floor, guys who built fully stocked shelters and had the weapons to defend them, and they were now predicting apocalypse. Most of the traders were pragmatic and didn't fear an economic apocalypse, but they didn't think the future was very promising either. It was unanimous that the days of the 1980's "greatest bull market ever" were finished and that it would be a struggle to make a living on the floor for the foreseeable future. Nobody dreamed that the great technology bull market of the 1990's would bring exponentially more opportunity to the PSE than ever before, that our volumes would grow more than one thousand percent in the next six years, and that our focus on technology listings in the eighties would make us a major options exchange in the nineties. I still doubted I would be there for the rest of 1987.

October turned to November and the market continued to stabilize. After the burst of activity during the crash however, volume had plummeted and showed no sign of returning. Finally, on the day before Thanksgiving, Bill approached me and said it was time to talk about my future. The market was slow so we stepped off the floor to talk. I was calm, my mind was still and whatever the outcome, I was happy that I would know my future. If the news was bad, I was ready to scour the city for a restaurant job that afternoon. I had never guessed that the useful experience from my college days would end up being from my service jobs.

Bill began by telling me what I already knew: the good times were done, volume would stay low and only the best traders would survive the lean years ahead. He told me he was worried about his own future.

"Half the market makers down here will be gone in six months," he rightly predicted.

The longer he talked, the more certain I became that he was laying me off, telling me to go back to college, to pursue a more stable career. He was taking his time, explaining the reasons, and letting me down easy; how else would he tell me my dream was dead? I felt the last of my hope evaporating,

"If I were you," Bill continued, "I would go back to college and then find a *real* job."

He paused for a few seconds and I held my breath. Finally, he said:

"But I told you I'd back you, so if you are dumb enough to still want to do it, I'll put the money up. We should be able to get you on a seat by February."

"Alright," was all I could say.

No Depression

I drove to Sacramento that afternoon to visit my parents for Thanksgiving. When I arrived, I again found Dad sitting alone in his favorite chair in a dimly lit room, with the dog at his feet and his cane under his hand. I dropped my things by the front door and joined him.

"I talked to Bill today," I said. "I am starting as a market maker on February 1."

Dad didn't respond right away; he sat there as if pondering what I had told him.

"Well, that sounds about right to me," he said.

Then he started asking questions about my experiences on the floor and my new life in San Francisco. He wanted to know everything. No detail was too small. We talked for hours about my few months on the floor. I didn't realize it at the time but we were establishing a custom that would continue for the next six years until his death. Every workday, around five o'clock at night, we would talk on the phone. I would tell him about my day on the floor, the trades I was made and what I was hoping would happen in the market. Though he didn't know enough about options to comment specifically on my trades, he would listen and give me bits of feedback and advice on everything else. This daily call was important to both of us; I needed someone to talk to about my trading and it allowed him to vicariously experience the exciting new life I was forging.

When I got back to work, the market was very slow; nobody wanted to think about their stock portfolio after the trauma of the crash. After December expiration, the floor was almost empty, most traders, including Bill, take an extended break for the holidays. I loved this, because I was responsible for managing his account while he was away. A young trader, Jonathan Armstrong, with whom I had watched some of the Marty O'Connor videos in an effort to stay awake, asked me to manage his account as well while he took his first vacation from trading. Jonathan was a high school dropout and one of the smartest traders I ever met and he went on to make a fortune trading options all over the world.

I watched both accounts with the focus of a neurosurgeon operating. Both Jonathan and Bill were *short vol* in Microsoft, which means they were short more option than they were long and hoping the stock would not move very much and that the relative price of the options would come down. If prices did come down, I had instructions to buy in the options they were short.

My status in the crowd had changed. Everyone knew I would be a trader soon and treated me with more respect. I was allowed to stand down *in* the pit, not at the back where the runners were which put me in a great position to ask the other traders about what they traded and why they traded it. Considering they were helping someone they knew would be a future competitor, the traders were very generous with their knowledge, answering every question I asked as best they could. This was ten times more valuable than the books and video I had been studying.

I did, however, have to learn what questions *not* to ask. One day I saw a trader named Rick O'Steen buy some calls and hedge them for what I thought was a bad price.

"Hey Rick?" I asked, "Why are you buying the 45 calls at that level?"

"Because I am an idiot," he said. "I panicked."

I talked to Jonathan and Bill on the telephone every day and they gave me specific volatility levels where they wanted to buy in the options they were short. Both of their accounts were doing well because the options were beginning to erode into the slow holiday period and there was very little for me to do.

Then, the week after Christmas, the price of volatility collapsed. Volatility is a measure of risk and the crash proved there was plenty of risk so prices had remained higher than normal since the crash. But in the few days after Christmas, with the market flat lining every day, volatility collapsed. Wednesday it opened down fifteen percent and was now *lower* than where they had said to buy it. I called them both but couldn't reach either one. I knew I had to act, because prices could go back up as quickly as they came down but was reluctant to trade in their accounts without specific permission. In addition, since I wasn't a member yet, I would have to hire a floor broker to trade the options and coordinate with him to make sure I could trade stock at the right price to hedge the options. This is called *leg risk*. Once you buy the options you are *legged* and if the stock falls before you can sell it the trade becomes bad. Handling leg risk was difficult working alone, having to coordinate with a broker made it even harder.

I decided to work with an independent broker in Microsoft named Sol Haberman and nervously explained to him what I needed to do.

"No problem, kid," he said. "Just listen to Uncle Sol and we'll get it done. I do this all the time."

I watched every tick of Microsoft that day and saw that Sol always traded when the market was in our favor. We ended up trading at *better* prices than we needed, making Jonathon and Bill more money.

Jonathon came back before New Year's Eve and was pleased with what I had done. He gave me a crisp fifty-dollar bill for my efforts. Rather than deposit it in my bank, which was across the street from the exchange, I took it home that night so I could see it sitting with my wallet and keys on my nightstand (which at that point was an old cardboard box wrapped in several pages of the San Francisco Chronicle's Sporting Green sports page). I went out with some new friends from the trading floor to a New Year's Eve party, but even amongst the celebrations and festivity in anticipation of January first, all I could think about was February first.

Back to work after the New Year and, for the second time, was it was my last month as a clerk. I put the thought of another delay out of my mind and continued my preparations. I still hardly knew anyone in San Francisco, and had turned down the few social invitations I did get. It wasn't the time I didn't want to spare, but the focus; I didn't want to think of anything other than options. On January 15th, BTR Trading was officially approved as a trading entity with me as its sole trader. I signed a contract to lease an exchange seat beginning February first. If I was born to run, now was the time to get my stride.

Finally, it was the weekend before my first day as an Options Market Maker on the floor of the Pacific Stock Exchange. Friday night I already felt like I was going to come out of my skin with anticipation and began willing the weekend to be over. I couldn't sleep Friday night, tossing and turning before getting up at my normal workday time of four in the morning. Sitting in my quiet apartment reading a day-old newspaper, the walls felt closer every time I looked up. I realized that this would to be the longest weekend of my life if I stayed in my apartment, so I decided to spend both days exploring my new hometown.

I left my apartment before eight o'clock in the morning and felt moisture in the air as I stepped out into a grey winter northern California day. I walked up Franklin Street to Bush and turned right toward downtown. I walked over Russian Hill and down to the

Exchange building in the Financial District. Arriving at the bottom of Bush Street, I looked at the entrance to the building that held the options floor and suddenly it seemed insane to think I could walk through that door and compete with experienced traders a decade older than me. I was twenty-one years old and only ten months earlier I hadn't even known what an option was. The longer I stood there looking at the exchange, the harder it became to breathe. I walked down to the Bay Bridge and stood underneath it. I would return to this spot many times in my career to meditate on difficult days. Then the sun began to break through the overcast sky in rays of light and my perspective shifted. Maybe I could succeed on the floor. This had to be the right decision -- I had never felt so certain of anything. I would walk onto that floor Monday and begin a long and successful career trading options, I told myself. One day I would be the biggest trader on the floor. Maybe I would even be an Exchange Governor.

Leaving the bridge, I walked a few miles down the Embarcadero, past the Ferry Terminal and Pier 39, to Fisherman's Wharf to have lunch at Alioto's Seafood. Alioto's had become a tourist trap and the food was not very good but it was the first restaurant my dad had taken me to in San Francisco so it felt perfect. After lunch I continued along the bay front, through Fort Mason and the Marina, all the way out to the Golden Gate Bridge. From there I headed back up the steep San Francisco hills to Pacific Heights and marveled at the mansions at the top of the hill before walking downhill back to my apartment. It was dark by the time I got home, so I stopped at the corner deli and bought a sandwich for dinner.

I slept better that night and didn't wake up until after six, but when I did the apartment walls immediately started closing in on me again. San Francisco is a small city, seven miles by seven miles, and I had covered a lot of it Saturday so I decided to drive north over the Golden Gate Bridge to Marin County and hike up Mt. Tamalpais. I drove to Mill Valley and found the trailhead just outside of town. Railroad Grade is a trail that follows the path of the old railcar that used to take tourists to the top. *Tam*, as the locals call it, is a 2,500-foot mountain in the middle of Marin County, which provides breathtaking 360-degree view of ocean, bay and city. Hiking up the grade that day, I pictured myself as a successful market maker, a member of a trading crowd, managing a portfolio of options while making a fair and orderly market. I imagined myself gaining experience, learning, growing and becoming a leading trader in the crowd. I didn't dream about making money, only making market. When I reached the top of Tam, I looked out over the San Francisco Bay and saw the buildings of the financial district reflecting the midday sun like a beacon. I stayed on the summit for a couple of hours, breathing in the grandeur, before slowly hiking back to the bottom.

On Monday morning I woke up at three o'clock, pleased that I had slept that long. I stayed in bed for another hour and went over everything I had learned one last time. Then I got up and took a long shower and slowly got ready. This was the one day I had nothing to do until the market opened, no trades from the previous day to clear and no position to analyze. I felt like I had killed a lot of time showering but was still in the office by five. I made myself wait until five-thirty before I put on my new trading jacket and clipped my temporary trading badge proudly on my lapel. I was the first trader to arrive in the Microsoft pit, and stood there staring at my sheets as if there was some critical piece of information on them that would provide the key to my success. Truth was, the numbers were a blur -- I was just trying to pass the last minutes before the market opened and I would be a trader.

Finally, at six-thirty in the morning, as on every other weekday, the bell rang and the market opened. I felt every strike of the bell's reverberation as I gathered with the other market makers for the *opening rotation* - the process of opening all the option classes in our pit as quickly as possible. I did not participate in the rotation as it is a more difficult time to trade and I wanted to wait until the options were open and the market was stable to make my first trade.

As soon as the rotation was over, Bill turned and looked directly at me.

"What's your market on the March 80 call?" he asked.

Terrified, I checked the market and stammered:

"One bid, at a quarter."

"Sell you five," Bill said.

"Buy five," I said with a worried voice.

Bill wrote up his sell ticket and handed to me. I took it from him and stared at it wondering what he was doing. Before I could say or do anything, I heard:

"March 80s One and a quarter bid 5."

"Sold!" I said in a much stronger voice.

I made a quarter five times (which is $112.50) and had no risk. Bill was getting my *cherry* and giving me a profitable first trade. I stood looking at him unable to express the gratitude I felt for this ritual and for everything he had done.

"Save that card," he said. "You're never gonna get me like that again."

Part II

First Noble Truth: "there is suffering"

"Now this...is the noble truth of suffering: birth is suffering, aging is suffering, illness is suffering, death is suffering; union with what is displeasing is suffering; separation from what is pleasing is suffering; not to get what one wants is suffering; in brief, the five aggregates subject to clinging are suffering."

"Your father and I are so proud of you, Robert," my mother is standing on the deck of my new home in the hills of Marin County, north of San Francisco, a few miles from Mt. Tam. She's smiling as she says, "and this house! It just amazes me every time we visit!"

It is a crisp, sunny, Northern California winter day. Christmas, 1993. My new house sits on the northern slope of Madrone Canyon. The trees are gently waving in the breeze, a deep green in the sharp winter sunlight, birds glide in circles above it all. My mom raves about the house and my career. And every word feels like a blow. To the head and to the body.

I had been trading for almost six years with considerable success. I had bought the house in February and gotten married in August that year, so this Christmas should have been a happy time. But between the money I had put into the house (I did not want a big monthly mortgage so the down payment was significant) and the cost of getting married and starting a household, my trading capital was lower than I liked it to be when I returned from my honeymoon in September. It had been a very good year until then though, so I trusted it would continue and I would soon make enough money to increase my working capital back to a comfortable level.

LEAP options had been introduced in January of that year. *LEAPS* are longer-dated options, two or three years in term, as opposed to standard listed options, which are one to twelve months in duration. Options trading is a bet on *mean reversion*, which means that you look back over the history of pricing in an option, and take the average, or *mean*, of how it behaves; then, when the pricing gets far enough above or below that mean, you put the trade on, betting that the price will revert back. Options are priced in relation to an underlying stock, and the pricing of that relationship is considered the *implied volatility* of that option because it is what the market implies. Options on stocks that do not have many price swings are cheaper than those on stocks that move around every session. Income stocks, like utilities and large conglomerates, that have consistent revenue and earnings, trade at a lower *implied volatility* than *growth* stocks, like a new internet company or a biotech. Normally, we could look back at volatility data in a specific option and see how it had been priced (*implied vol*) and how it had actually moved (*historical vol*). When the implied is lower than the historical, the option was a good one to be long: when the implied is higher, the option is a good one to be short. Sounds easy? It's not. The trick is that a *historical volatility* is just that, historical, and though the future often imitates the past, sometimes it doesn't. In trading the LEAPS, we didn't have this historical data to use in trying to predict the vols.

I had tried to approach trading LEAPS that year cautiously, but where there was greater uncertainty in the pricing, there was also greater opportunity for reward. One of the first market axioms I noticed applied not only to trading and finance, but to most things: *where there is more risk there is more (potential) reward.* When the LEAPS were listed we priced them at what we thought at the time was low, thinking there would naturally be more sellers in the market. We were right about the sellers, it seemed like every order to trade LEAPS was a seller, and the crowd quickly built an inventory of the long-dated options. We were wrong about our pricing though, what we thought was low was soon higher than our offer, where we *hoped* to sell them. From the first day, we lowered the volatility quickly (causing losses on our positions), but the sellers continued hitting our lowered bids and we continued lowering them. Through August I had managed to offset the losses in the LEAPS with my other positions and trading so I was not too worried.

I returned from my honeymoon and soon I (and the rest of the market makers) had bought all that we could risk to be long. When the selling continued, all we could do was lower the markets and accept the losses. Although I had thought I was being cautious with my trading, the long-dated options were higher in nominal value and I lost more money per contract than I ever had. In September I lost twenty-five percent of my capital on my LEAPS position, and, this time, was unable to offset much of it with my other trading activity. It was the first significant losing month of my career.

October wasn't much better. The LEAP sellers stopped hitting our bids so the LEAPS did stop going down, but there was no sign of demand materializing so we could make a little capital back and get out of our losing positions. I redoubled my efforts in trading the standard options, but, in doing so, tried to do too much, and was unable to make money back that way either. I noticed a small ball of stress that was just starting to take hold in my chest.

Heading into November, I managed to convince myself that the LEAPS *couldn't go any lower*. I was still young enough to not know that ninety-nine out of one hundred times you say this to yourself, you are wrong. Usually very wrong. But that November I convinced myself that even if the LEAPS weren't going to move back up, they weren't going any lower either. Reviewing my subpar trading activity, I saw that I had gotten away from the things I do well and had started swinging for the fences in an attempt to make back what I'd lost. Bill had taught me trading through sports analogies and my favorite was the *Charlie Lau Theory of Hitting*. Charlie Lau was a major league hitting coach who taught players to go with the pitch that was thrown: a low fastball you try to hit back up the middle for a single, an outside pitch you hit into the opposite field with less power, and only when you see a hanging curveball up over the plate do you swing for the fences. I had been trying to hit everything out of the park.

The first week of November went by with no improvement in my results despite my analysis. At least the LEAPS *had* stopped going down, and my losses were small. Gaining confidence and wanting to gauge the market, we raised out markets a little, by the minimum increment, a quarter of a dollar higher. Within minutes the sellers were back. They hit our higher bids. Then hit the bids at our original level, then lower, and lower; and finally left more offered at the lowest price forcing us to lower the bid further (and our capital with it). As the bell rang, I knew my account would look bad the next morning. The ball of anxiety became a fist.

The next morning the news was as bad as I'd feared: My account was down a whopping forty percent. All the way back to thirty thousand dollars. Right where I'd started. The fist gripped harder and began to twist. Later that day, I got a 'tap'. On the floor, a *tap* is when the risk manager at your clearing firms sends a clerk to summon you to their office; they politely tap you on the shoulder and tell you that you must go straight to the risk office before making any trades. Although I had reduced my positions and capital usage somewhat, the abrupt loss in capital left me with too little to support the risk in my portfolio. Every account has what is called a *haircut*, which is the amount of money that it cost to hold both the position and the risk in the account. Clearing firms will loan you money against your capital so you don't have to have enough to cover the whole haircut, but they do not like to loan more than you have in the account; a 2:1 haircut-to-equity ratio. My loss took my ratio to 4:1. A couple of weeks earlier I would not have believed I would get a tap; I had sailed through my first five and half years of trading without hitting a single storm.

I went up to meet with my risk manager, Barbara Newton, who was the San Francisco branch manager for First Options of Chicago (FOC).

There was no receptionist outside her office so I poked my head in.

"Oh, hey, thanks for coming up," Barbara said as if I'd had a choice. "Come in and have a seat. How are things going today?"

"A little better," I lied.

"Your ratio was 4:1 coming in. We usually don't like to see it this high. Can you make a capital contribution? We'd really like to get it down to 2:1."

She was asking for thirty thousand dollars I didn't have.

"I can't," I said. "Everything is tied up in the house."

"How much is the house worth?" Barbara asked.

"Six hundred grand." I said.

"And how much is your mortgage?"

"I just paid it down to two hundred grand, that's why I don't have any cash," I said, adding, "I don't like to have debt."

She was making notes and didn't care about the explanation; she only cared how much they could get out of it if my account went into deficit.

"Okay, you can continue to trade," Barbara said. "But if you go above 6:1 you will be closing only."

She meant that if positions cost six times more than my capital I would only be allowed to make trades that reduced an open position. This means you can't actively try to make money back, you just have to wait and hope your positions turn around. For me this would mean coming into the pit every day hoping for a miracle LEAP buyer to emerge. Not many traders make it back from closing only without a capital injection. And no matter your ratio, if your capital got below fifteen thousand dollars, your account is immediately liquidated. Most of our positions were in illiquid options that are difficult to trade so when the clearing firm liquidates the position at one time it drives the prices of your options further against you. The other market makers usually already have the same position as you, so won't trade with you (adding to their problem) unless the price gets extreme. Often the cost of liquidation is (significantly) more than fifteen thousand dollars left in your account. If it is, you are not only out of a job, but also in debt to the clearing firm; which is why Barbara was asking about my house.

I left her office thinking I would have to find a partner to put money into my account. Of course, I would have to pay handsomely for someone to take this risk and would probably give up half my profits for years to come. Adjusting my hopes and dreams down, I went back to the one person who had ever invested in me.

I pulled Bill aside after the close.

"Hey, I hate to ask this, but I may need to raise some money, my account is almost gone. These LEAPS are killing me. Any chance you want to be partners again?" I asked, failing in an attempt to sound upbeat.

"Yeah, those LEAPS are killing me too," he said, shaking his head. "I was in Barbara's office yesterday."

I knew that meant there was no chance he could spare capital for me.

"Everyone I know is in the same boat," Bill continued before I could ask if he knew someone who might be interested.

It kept getting worse. By the end of November, I had lost another ten thousand dollars and was only five thousand above the 'blow out' line. The twisting in my gut was a permanent part of me now and I could feel it in my chest too. Every day in December, I arrived at work hoping my luck would turn, that I would make some good trades and start the long climb back. Every day I went home disappointed with the fist inside me twisting a little more. By that Christmas afternoon with my mom, I was barely above the line, one more move down in the LEAPS and I was done.

The praise from my mom made it hard to breathe.

I hadn't told anyone except Bill how dire my situation was. My wife knew I wasn't doing as well as I had, but I never let her see how bad our situation was, there was no need to force her to share my worries. I told myself I couldn't talk to anyone about it, because it is impolite to discuss money. I burned with shame whenever I thought of discussing it with anyone. I think my father suspected it wasn't going well, but I was vague, and he didn't press. The day after Christmas I went on a mountain bike ride with my good friend Dave, and, after discussing his own career with me, he asked how mine was going. The quickness and certainty of my response (*Great!*) made me realize I was clinging to something more than just the money. I was attached to people thinking of me as a gifted young trader with the magic touch, whose career went only upward, and who never needed anybody's help.

Second Noble Truth: "we create our own suffering"

"The Second Noble Truth is the truth of the origin or causes of suffering. Though the mind itself is the ultimate cause, there are three main categories of suffering... Attachment, Anger, and Ignorance."

That Christmas night I fell into bed too tired to sleep. Not from the mountain bike ride, but from the effort it took to hide my fear and anxiety. The fist gripping my insides now filled my entire body and was *physically* overwhelming. My mind raced on a closed course of pain, fear, and shame, through images of my house for sale, me jobless, a failure at my first career, everybody saying *we knew he wasn't that good*.

But in the darkness that night I found a tiny light and I grabbed it and held on as tightly as I could for it occurred to me that the new year was coming and I was certain that would change everything. I was certain that this storm would finally end. Trading would return to the way it had been for my first five years and the money would again accumulate in my account. The struggle would soon seem as distant as a winter storm does on a hot summer day. There would always be bad days, but they would be infrequent and less severe. I could feel how I would slowly forget the knot in my guts and turn the experience into a cautionary tale; how it would become a story I tell about the pressures a trader has to bear. All I had to do was survive this last week of the year. The grip that was twisting my insides loosened a little as I considered this ray of hope, and I rolled over and had the best night of sleep I had gotten in weeks.

That week, I balanced precariously on the hope that the New Year would (somehow) change everything back and return me to my life as a hot shot options trader. Nothing ever happens in the markets between Christmas and New Year's Day, so it was easy enough to glide into my imagined promised land.

I arrived an hour early for work on January 3rd, excited to get the market opened and begin to trade my way back. I had taken my trading jacket home with me over the holiday weekend and stripped it of every pin, badge and decoration, emptied everything from every pocket, and threw all of it (except my required Exchange badges) into the garbage. I had wanted to trash the coat too but could not afford to pay for a new one so I washed it twice instead. In my office I now restocked the pockets with trading tickets, a calculator, note cards, and three pens. I clipped my exchange badges back onto the lapel, packed my daily trading sheets in the appropriate pockets, and headed for the floor earlier than I had since my first year of trading.

The market opened that day as any other and it quickly became apparent that the vagaries of the market did not care about the calendar change. Nothing was different. With every hour that went by without whatever it was I was expecting to happen not happening the grip on my gut started to increase again. I fought it off with optimistic thoughts for a day or two but by the end of the first week of the year it was as tight as it had ever been.

Another week went by with no improvement and it felt like I couldn't take a deep enough breath to satisfy my need for oxygen. I was still one bad mark from being closed out and there was no one to ask for help. The next week was January expiration and I had big positions, it would offer opportunities to make some money if I could just have a little luck. I did not have any. After expiration I was still only a few hundred dollars above the line. January was basically over, and there hadn't even been sign of anything improving.

Third Noble Truth: "we can release ourselves from our suffering"

"The one who has conquered himself is a far greater hero than he who has defeated a thousand men a thousand times."

That Sunday night I was a wreck: I wanted the weekend to both last forever and be over immediately. I had tried all the things I usually did to relieve stress: mountain biking, watching a sports game, drinking… everything seemed to make it worse. The phone rang and I answered it just to have something to do. It was my new father-in-law, Jim French, calling. Jim had been an options trader on the Pacific after a career as a professional baseball player, and we had always gotten along well. I was glad to talk to him and stop the looping in my mind for a few minutes. Soon the talk came around to trading.

"How's it going on the floor?" he asked. "I hear it's been tough down there."

I almost began my usual vague answer to deflect a real conversation but something made me stop.

"Terrible, actually," I said. "It's been a rough six months."

As soon as I spoke the words I began to regret it, a voice in my head screaming, *You told your father-in-law?* I waited for the worst, for some kind of admonition.

"Dammit," he said. "How bad is it?"

The tale of my situation poured out of me for the next five minutes, and with every second that went by, the fist loosened its grip a little bit. I finished by saying I didn't know if I could make it back, I might *blow out.*

"Blow out or not, you're gonna be fine," he said. "You've got talent. Every trader goes through this. Even the best. Every great l trader I know has a story like yours: Nothing goes right, every trade feels doomed, good trades turn out bad and bad trades turn out worse. Try everything, nothing works and it feels like you'll never make money again. Down to your last."

It sure sounded like my situation. Instantly, I felt better.

"And then, one day, for no reason, it goes the other way," he said, adding, "and you'll be fine kid."

When he finished, I thanked him profusely. It was after we had hung up that I realized he had probably called to speak to his daughter, but I was in a hurry to make another call. Immediately after hanging up with Jim, I called my good friend, David Haynes.

"Remember on our bike ride I told you that work was going well?" I said. "Well, it's not. I'm damn near out of business and don't know if I can make it back. I might lose the house and everything,"

"Oh, man, that blows," he replied. "You can crash here if you need a place to stay. Hey! You want to come up Tahoe next weekend? Come to Tahoe and stay with us! Skiing always soothes the soul."

"Thanks, man," I said, exhaling with relief at having gotten it off my chest. "Yeah. You know what? I'd love to join you in Tahoe."

The next number I dialed was my dad's. His health was deteriorating ever more rapidly (he would die a few months later) and I had been afraid to upset him with any bad news. He answered and the story of the last six months poured out of me. I didn't stop talking for ten minutes. I told him about the LEAPS and putting more money into the house. I explained how the rest of my trading had inexplicably turned sour with every break seeming to go against me and that I had been forced to pledge my house as equity against my risk and could very well lose it. I told him how I had learned a hard lesson about trying to make it all back in a day or week or month and was now just taking it day to day, trying to stay in business and make a little money doing the things that I had done well in the past.

Even before I finished talking I felt the fist in my chest let go completely. I could breathe easily for the first time in months. In telling my father what had happened and how I'd handled it, I realized I was doing everything I possibly could. When I finally gave him a chance to speak, my father said,

"Well, it sounds like you're doing everything you can," putting into words the thought that had crossed my own mind only moments before. Then, almost with a shrug in his voice, he added, "it'll turn around."

And, as it turned out, he was right.

In fact, it turned around almost immediately: I doubled my capital the following week. And, although this was only a part of what I needed to do, I gained more than capital that week: I got my confidence back. The next three months were the best I ever had and the year was twice as good as any I had experienced before.

The Eightfold Noble Path

Wise View

Wise Intention

Wise Speech

Wise Conduct

Wise Livelihood

Wise Effort

Wise Mindfulness

Wise Concentration

The Eightfold Noble Path

Although the first noble truth teaches us there is suffering, Buddha didn't leave us alone to suffer through life. His teachings on the avoidance of suffering is called the *Eightfold Noble Path*, a collection of lessons that provide guidance on how to live and prosper among (and in some cases in spite of) the suffering that surrounds us. The Eightfold Noble Path teaches us ways to let go of suffering, ways to become our best selves. In the following chapters, stories from my trading career illuminate how and why I chose to walk the path and how, in the end, I found Buddha on the trading floor.

Wise View

[All of the eight noble paths are important, but wise view is critical because without it you cannot walk any of the others.]

"Wise view is no view. In wise view there is no point of view because we see things as they are, without judgment, and from all points of view. Wise view is seeing the world as it presents itself and not through the lens of any religion, belief structure or political party."

As a market maker, you are required to make a two-sided market: a bid and an offer providing supply or demand, as the market needs. As a reward for this, a market maker is allowed to *capture the spread*, by selling at a higher price (the offer) than where he buys (the bid). When I hear the term *capture the spread* in the financial press it sounds like every time we sell on the offer another customer appears to sell the option back to us on the bid leaving us with no position and a profit in the account. Oh, were it that easy.

Although it does happen (in my decades as a trader I was able to capture the spread a handful of times), it is more like a unicorn than a common house cat. The other 99.9% of the time, when a customer pays your offer or sells on your bid, you have to hedge the transaction in the short term in order to lock in its value in volatility (the relationship between the price of the option and the stock). The only place we had an edge in the market was in trading this volatility relationship, so we tried to take the direction of the underlying stock out of the equation with what is termed *delta neutral hedging*. Just as we spent all of our time pricing volatility, there were many more who spent their time pricing stocks and we wanted to let them bet on the direction of the stock while we bet on the volatility relationship. This meant buying or selling the underlying stock in the short-term market to hedge the option. Hence, *delta neutral hedging*.

If someone claims to be able to consistently predict long-term moves in the market, you should be skeptical and examine their track record carefully. But if someone claims they can predict the shortest-term fluctuations, they are either extremely rich or they're lying. When people tried to sell me systems to predict short-term market fluctuations I knew it didn't work. On the floor, our time frame was "immediately or sooner" and for good reason: we wanted to hedge the options and get back to making markets where we had our edge. We were in the business of trading risk, not of trading assets, and risk was what we knew. A long-term investor can do fundamental analysis of a company's business, financials, events and strategy and make predictions how that company will fare over time. None of that means anything in the short-term market and rationalizing a short-term position with a company's long-term promise is a fool's game. It's like betting on the team with the best record in the league to win a game even though they are trailing by twenty points with less than a minute to go. Long-term thinking is as damaging to a trader's performance as short-term thinking is to an investor's.

In 2008, when the stock market fell and fell and fell, I got a lot of calls from friends who were horrified that their IRA's and Mutual Funds and stocks were worth a lot less than they had paid for them. Most of my calls were from friends in their early forties, as was I at the time, and what they had been building for at least a decade – their retirement savings -- was now gone. By the time they called me they were traumatized from the declining nest egg and ready to do anything to stop the pain. I usually hesitate to give financial advice to friends but at that time I gave some forceful and specific advice:

"The next time your account statement arrives in the mail," I would begin slowly, "I want you to immediately and thoroughly destroy it before you even open the envelope. If you have a shredder use it, otherwise burn it in your fireplace or tear it into tiny pieces and throw it away."

They usually interrupted with protestations of worry but I explained calmly,

"You are twenty years away from using your retirement money. You made these investments knowing that so don't let this (short term) trauma affect those (long term) decisions."

Because my friends knew I was a very active trader they were surprised by my advice.

"Come on, you told me you have traded more at work this month than you usually do in a quarter!" one friend said, "I *know* you're making money, man. Why won't you tell me what to do?"

To which I replied: "I am trading actively at work, that's true, but I haven't opened my IRA statement in a year."

I have interviewed, evaluated and hired dozens of traders in my career. Identifying potentially successful traders is very difficult; traders are a diverse group, there's no tangible way to predict who will thrive and who will dive. Many of the requisite skills are tough to measure or quantify and the required ability to use multiple skills concurrently under pressure is nearly impossible to evaluate. If someone made it through the screening process to an interview with me they definitely had the math skills necessary to price options and expert knowledge of options strategy. If I ran them through a mock trading situation they could price the options and identify the best trade available. Most could even do it fast enough to compete on the floor. But could they do it in a volatile market with real money at risk, a broker barking in their face, and markets makers boxing them out like Dennis Rodman going for a rebound in the NBA Finals?

And even if you *do* find a qualified candidate you think can handle all that and still trade with a wise view; will they be able to do it after ten days in a row of making money? What about ten consecutive days of losing money? Divorce? Loss of a loved one? Illness?

As one of my teachers said:

"It's easy to have wise view in the temple, but will you have it in the fire?"

I once hired a trader named Bill Thomas to make markets on the CBOE. Bill did as well as anybody had throughout training and looked like a lock to be a solid producer on the floor. He had a quickness of mind and an ability to think creatively - a rare combination - and I was sure he would be the star of his training class. After nine months training and clerking on the CBOE, Bill's first day of trading arrived.

He didn't make it to the closing bell.

I was in our LMM post in San Francisco when the phone rang:

"Kovell."

"Bill Thomas quit," Matt Ziol, our head trader and office manager in Chicago, explained that Bill "got hazed in the pit and froze."

"He started stammering to a broker and the crowd eviscerated him," I could tell Matt was shaking his head at Thomas' fatal misstep. Never let them see you sweat – it's a cliché for a reason. Still…

"He quit?"

I couldn't believe what he was telling me.

"Did you talk to him?" I asked.

"Nope," Matt answered. "Andrew was up in the office taking a break when Bill came up. He said Bill was shaking and so choked up and could barely speak. He just said *I'm done. I'm sorry but I'm done* then he got all his stuff and left."

When I finally spoke to Bill Thomas the next day I could tell right away he was never coming back.

I developed my own interview style to try to evaluate all of this. I asked questions rapidly, sometimes interrupting an answer to move on and other times staying silent long after the candidate finished. The best candidates would stare back with the same look and wait for the next question. My questions varied greatly, from options theory and mathematics to pop culture and philosophy; subject-wise, I made a point to ask them in random order.

For instance, I might ask a candidate:

"Why do you want to be a trader?"

Then,

"What is the expected vol of a twenty percent downside put if the ATM is trading thirty and the thirty-day historical is twenty-two?"

Followed by:

"What is your favorite movie?"

And,

"Do you like to gamble? Favorite food? In three words tell me the meaning of life. What is the fair value of the Dow Jones Industrial Average?"

Of course, most of these questions don't necessarily have correct answers – I was looking for candidates who answered honestly rather than with what they thought I wanted to hear. For instance, answering *options market making* when asked to define the meaning of life using only three words caused an immediate end to the interview and dismissal of the candidate.

The most important question I posed candidates was the last one I mentioned above: what is the fair value of the Dow Jones Industrial Average? This question actually does have a right answer and what that answer demonstrates is a *wise view*. Not many candidates got it right but any who did ended up becoming successful traders. The answer I was seeking had nothing to do with market theory, stock valuation, price-to-earnings ratios, wave theory, chaos theory, or any other theory. In fact, the more words used to explain an answer the more imaginary points I deducted. The answer I was looking for was *wherever it last traded*.

When I worked for PEAK6, the firm had its best traders take detailed personality evaluations in order to find traits that were common to the group. The results were more varied than a random sampling of complete strangers so the personality evaluations ultimately offered no help.

I hired all of our traders in San Francisco and our trainees turned into successful traders twice as often as in the other offices. What was it I was looking for that may have caused our hires to outperform?

Experience is highly valued in modern society. A cursory look through job-posting sites will reveal that a minimum of five to ten years of experience is a prerequisite for the majority of offers. By those standards, for most of my career on the floor I was unqualified technically or I lacked the experience necessary to even secure employment on the floor. And yet before I was thirty years old I was running one of the largest options pits in the country, trading the most volatile and active stocks of all time while also serving as Vice Chairman of the Pacific Stock Exchange.

"He doesn't have the experience it takes to handle this volume and volatility," I imagined my detractors saying. "It's only a matter a time before his luck runs out."

Experience is an asset, but one that is as overvalued as a Mortgage fund in 2007. Experience is a *view,* it allows us to focus in and understand our job by showing us how things happen in the real world. It took some experience to understand the trading floor and its machinations and to see the order amongst the chaos. Experience is like putting on a pair of glasses' it brings everything viewed through it into focus but narrows your view to what you can see through the lenses. With a little experience you begin to understand what you are doing and your performance improves. More experience, more improvement. It's not a straight trajectory, though. Experience can sometimes give us false confidence which in turns begets an unwise view that can hinder us more than the breadth of our experience helped.

Think of your *experience* as being a pair of glasses you put on to better focus on work. Now imagine that as your experience grows so, too, do the glasses. With each certainty achieved from *experience*, the lenses grow outward, like pipes, from each eye. And when we look through a pipe, we can focus intensely on a single area in our field of view. We can see it better than any*thing* or any*body* else. But here is the flaw: that narrow pipe blocks out the rest of the world and the longer the pipe grows to be, the less we see around us.

The most valuable lesson I learned from decades of trading experience is that I know very little. There are plenty of careers where every day goes the same and at some point you've seen it all, but most jobs are like trading and are always evolving; sometimes slowly and at other times, with a shock. Most of the time events play out in recognizable patterns and experience will guide you through with the advantage of having been there before. But when things don't go according to plan, experience becomes as detrimental to your pattern of thinking as wearing glasses with long pipes attached to the lenses would be to your field of vision. Both prevent you from recognizing changes that can and should be at the very least considered. And it is usually at times of great upheaval that risk and reward are highest.

*   *   *

I grew up rooting for the San Francisco Giants and throughout my childhood they were terrible. The most exciting thing they did was knock the Dodgers out of the playoffs in 1982 when Joe Morgan, near the end of his career, homered late in the final game of the year to complete a come from behind victory that meant nothing for the last place Giants but cost the Dodgers the division title.

In 1989, the San Francisco Giants won the National League pennant for the first time in twenty-seven years and I was thrilled. Even when they lost the first two games of the World Series in Oakland, I remained absolutely positive the Giants would win the series. I was one hundred percent certain of it. But at around five o'clock in the evening, just before the start of what would have been the first World Series game at Candlestick Park, the Loma Prieta earthquake rocked the Bay Area. The stadium was evacuated and the game was postponed. The Exchange was unable to open due to damage so we flew to New York to trade on the American Stock Exchange options floor while repairs were made. We traded there for three days before returning to our floor in San Francisco. After such a harrowing natural disaster, when the World Series resumed it seemed utterly unimportant. The Giants were quickly swept while the city repaired itself.

So, in 2002, when the San Francisco Giants made it back to the World Series and were leading three games to two in the series and 5-0 in the seventh inning of game six, I thought I would finally get to celebrate a World Series Championship. I was surrounded by all my Giants-fan-friends at a classic San Francisco bar called Shanghai Kelly's, getting ready to order a victory round of drinks when the Angels came to bat in the seventh inning. After the first batter was retired, Troy Glaus and Brad Fullmer hit back-to-back singles to give the Angels two base runners. Not a problem with a five-run lead, a home run would still leave the Angels trailing by two and we had our hottest pitcher, Russ Ortiz, on the mound. Ortiz had been on fire for the second half of the season and the playoffs and was credited for getting the Giants to the World Series in the first place.

But just before the next batter took the plate, Giants manager Dusty Baker emerged from the dugout and walked to the mound to remove Ortiz from the game. The Giants had a strong bullpen that year and one of its stars, Felix Rodriguez, was warmed up and ready to pitch. It wasn't a move Baker would have made during the season: Ortiz was pitching well and had only surrendered a couple of weak singles, but this was the World Series. Why not use your bullpen stars to close the game as if it were 1-0 instead of 5-0? The answer came when Scott Spezio hit a three-run home run off of the great Giants bullpen. Three more runs off the Giant's bullpen in the eighth won the game for the Angels. Game 7 was never close. A dispirited Giants team lost 4-1.

Dusty Baker was let go after the season and the Giants wouldn't get their World Series title for another eight years when, in 2010, they won their first of three championships in five years. Days after leaving the Giants, Baker was hired to manage the Chicago Cubs and unlike the Giants, was back in the playoffs the following season. Incredibly, the Cubs took a 3-2 series lead and then a 3-0 lead after seven innings of Game six with their hottest pitcher, Mark Prior, on the mound. Most people would praise Baker for drawing on his experience and leaving his starting pitcher in the game rather than risk bringing in a relief pitcher. A wise view, however, would be to evaluate this decision based only on what is happening in the game. When Prior gave up a one-out double to Juan Pierre in the eighth inning Baker didn't move from his place in the dugout. The next batter, Luis Castillo worked the count to three balls and two strikes and then fouled off eight pitches in a row to keep the at-bat alive. The eighth of these was a foul pop to the left side and just out of play. Moises Alou gave chase and was able to reach into the stands and get his mitt under the falling ball but the ball never made it into Alou's mitt. In his excitement to catch a foul ball at a playoff baseball game, a Cub's fan named Steve Bartman forgot to consider that Alou might be able to catch the ball for the second out of the inning. Bartman reached up and caught the ball…just above Alou's mitt.

After a long argument between Baker and the umpires, the play stood as a foul ball "out-of-play" and the count to Castillo remained three balls and two strikes. Fan interference can only be called if the fan reaches into the field of play and interferes. Perhaps due to the interruption or from frustration with the call, Prior threw his next pitch wildly and the catcher couldn't prevent it from going to the backstop, walking Castillo and allowing Pierre to advance to third base. All eyes were on the Cub's dugout looking for Baker to emerge and bring in a relief pitcher. He didn't. Baker's experience from the previous year must have been in his mind: whether or not it was the decisive reason he left Prior in the game we can never know. The Cubs went on to lose the series and Steve Bartman became persona-non-grata in Chicago.

In 2002, a friend I met on the board of my daughter's school introduced me to a place called The Center for Attitudinal Healing. The Center's mission is to provide peer support groups both for kids with cancer and other life-threatening diseases and for their parents and caregivers. They also have support groups for children of parents with life threatening illnesses and for many other groups facing a myriad of challenges. A *peer support group* is a gathering of people who face a similar adversity (such as kids battling cancer). With the help of a facilitator, participants share their experiences and struggles in order to support each other. The efficacy is easy to see when you watch a ten-year-old cancer patient light up with pride because he is able to comfort an anxious eight-year-old patient about to start chemotherapy.

"It kinda stinks most of the time, but then you feel better," the older patient might say. "Plus, they give you lots of toys and anything you want to eat."

I was inspired by the work of the center and decided to work as a volunteer. I started by taking the required facilitator training course. The job of the facilitator is not to be a group therapist or group leader, the point being discussions aren't led as much as they are simply facilitated. The therapy, the leading, happens between the members of the group. The facilitator is there only to assist when necessary and to assure the discussion stays within the principles of "attitudinal healing," which are read at the beginning of every meeting:

1. The essence of our being is love.
2. Health is inner peace. Healing is letting go of fear.
3. Giving and receiving are the same.
4. We can let go of the past and the future.
5. Now is the only time there is and each instant is for giving.
6. We can learn to love ourselves and others by forgiving rather than judging.
7. We can become love finders rather than fault finders.

8. We can choose and direct ourselves to be peaceful inside regardless of what is happening outside.
9. We are students and teachers to each other.
10. We can focus on the whole of life rather than the fragments.
11. Since love is eternal, death need not be viewed as fearful.
12. We can always perceive ourselves and others as either extending love or giving a call for help.

Training started at seven-thirty on a Saturday morning, a veritable lazy sleep-in as far as I was concerned. Not for most of my classmates. Most of them rushed in right at seven-thirty, carrying various sizes of coffees. The teacher talked for about ninety minutes reviewing the mission of the Center and the principles of Attitudinal Healing. As their coffee kicked in, most of my classmates came to life and listened attentively; however, one gentleman in his fifties who was sitting directly across from me did not. He was sound asleep. He wasn't snoring or drooling or slumping over but he was clearly asleep and for some reason it really aggravated me.

He had slept through most of the opening ninety minutes and I fumed about it so neither of us heard the wisdom being shared. I thought he was being disrespectful to the teacher, the rest of the students and to me. I sat there watching him sleep and wondering how many other people were doing the same and if the teacher would say anything. I fantasized about the person next to him abruptly waking him and then I started wishing my fourth-grade teacher, Mrs. Massey, could materialize, quietly creep up behind the sleeping man and then loudly clap her hands together like she used to do in elementary school.

As our first break approached, I found myself hoping the man would stay asleep through until the end of the session just so he could experience shock and embarrassment. But he woke up just as the session ended and wandered out of the room sleepily. When we went back in after the break I took my seat and was truly surprised to see "the sleeper" stumble back in with a cup of coffee.

"About time," I muttered too quietly for anyone to hear.

When the teacher started the next session, she asked us to go around the circle and introduce ourselves, to say where we are from and a little about ourselves and why we were there for training. As my fellow students introduced themselves I was focused on what I would say when my turn came, not on what they were saying about themselves. When it was "the sleeper's" turn, though, I was riveted. I couldn't wait to hear what he had to say for himself.

"Hi, I'm Tom," he said. "I'm from San Rafael and I am *really tired* this morning."

He didn't sound ashamed or even embarrassed for sleeping through the first hour and a half of training! This infuriated me. Furthermore, he clearly wasn't going to apologize. I couldn't wait to hear what had inspired *this guy* to come here and sleep through training.

"Last night was hard," Tom-the-sleeper continued. "Carol, that's my wife, she had a bad night. She has cancer, see, and is on home hospice and I'm taking care of her. I just can't watch a nurse handle her, you know? She has some good nights and she really wanted last night to be one of them because she knew how much this meeting…she knows what coming here today meant to me. She was suffering so much."

His laugh was wistful: "She was telling me she was fine. She said I should go to sleep even though we both knew how much she was suffering. She threw up on herself because she couldn't reach the toilet."

Wise Intention

"What we think, we become. We must resolve to be always willing to change and grow. To always work towards the cessation of things that we know harm others or us. With Wise Intention we are always trying to be better at everything we do. We live with the intention to leave every place we go, and everyone we meet, better than we found them. We believe in the things we do and the people we surround ourselves with and do everything we can to create the world around us that we desire."

One of my dad's favorite sayings was "better lucky than smart."

But in trading, you need to be both.

Throughout my trading career, there were many times where I benefited from good luck. Sometimes, very good luck. Not just within the financial world, where luck was an important player every day, but on a macro level. By 1992, I had become one of the largest market makers in the Microsoft pit and was looking to expand my book by trading other stocks. I started making markets and many were the other stocks trading in my pit: Nike, Maxtor (a disk drive maker), Mentor Condoms (you can imagine the banter) and Micron Technology. Although Nike would become one of the most successful companies in the world a decade or so later, it was Micron that made me.

Micron options were listed on the American Stock Exchange (AMEX) and the Chicago Board Options Exchange (CBOE), as well as the PSE. The Pacific had a poor history competing with the bigger exchanges in Chicago and New York, averaging less than fifteen percent of the market in competitive issues. With one exception: Microsoft had been listed on both the AMEX and PSE, but through the efforts of a trader and floor governor named Terry Brookshire, the Pacific had garnered the preponderance of the order flow and the AMEX delisted the options. Why would they do this when even ten percent of the volume in Microsoft is more than a hundred percent in most stocks? Well, around the same time, the PSE delisted options on Intel Corporation where we were the minor player and the AMEX had the preponderance of the volume. This gave each exchange a valuable exclusive listing. The timing must have been a coincidence because if this were done as a deal, the Federal Trade Commission would have considered it illegal collusion.

Micron was Terry Brookshire's new project and he was competing for order flow in the same way he had in Microsoft. However, Micron traded on *two* other exchanges - the AMEX and the CBOE - and he had only had about fifty percent of the volume in those. One of the things Terry did to attract customers was to keep his markets tight with little spread between bid and offer. This reduction in margin kept most market makers from trading Micron. I started trading it more to help and learn from Terry than make a lot of money.

Terry was a Vice Chairman of the Board of Governors, one of the top market makers on the floor, and a good, kind man. He was trading in the Microsoft pit when I started as a runner and I had immediately identified him as someone I wanted to emulate. According to Exchange rules all members have equal status, but I could see that the other members treated Terry with respect and deference. Usually taciturn and quiet, when Terry did speak a cacophonous crowd would silence itself to hear his words.

In 1992, Terry was retiring from the floor to run the trading firm he had founded. Without his efforts and guarantees the Micron order flow coming to the PSE would quickly be re-routed to the bigger exchanges. Although I had been helping Terry with the trading duties long enough to learn his methods, I was only twenty-five and did not have the same resources or contacts. Terry generously offered to help me establish some key professional relationships and went about setting up a week of meetings in New York.

This was crucial, but I was more worried about resources, which in trading means capital. My career was booming along and I had built my trading capital to a comfortable and increasing level, but it was still a lot less than Terry had worked with. Traveling to New York and making promises would put me at risk of getting in over my head. Even with the best intentions things can change instantly and dramatically in the markets. Micron, however, was a six-dollar stock; a memory chipmaker that few people were interested in and so it traded little volume. The Boise, Idaho, company manufactures Dynamic Random Access Memory chips (DRAM), which are the simplest memory chips that go into a computer. DRAM chips are easy to make and thus traded like a commodity with violent price swings resulting from rapid changes in demand or supply. Micron was the lowest cost manufacturer but was often battered by large memory price implosions caused by new competition or slacking personal computer demand. Volume in Micron was concentrated around events: the semiconductor industry's monthly book-to-bill ratio, which measures supply and demand for chips, and the company's quarterly earnings reports. I yearned for the challenge and the opportunity to follow in Terry's footsteps. Considering Micron's low profile and volume, I decided I could take the risk.

I asked Terry to set up the trip.

On the plane to New York, I panicked. What was I doing taking a week off from trading Microsoft to build a business in an unknown and unattractive semiconductor stock? Was I taking an unwise risk just to try to be like my idol? Would I be able to keep the promises I was about to make to the most influential people in my industry? What the hell was I thinking? Had I been driving I would have turned the car around, but the plane flew on to John F Kennedy International Airport with me on it, like it or not. Other than an emergency sixty-hour visit after the 1989 San Francisco earthquake closed our exchange, it was my first time in New York City.

I took a taxi to the Royalton Hotel in Midtown, recommended to me by my worldly friend Cabot Caldwell. Cabot was a floor-broker for Merrill Lynch and was far and away the most sophisticated and stylish person on the PSE options floor. He laughed when I had told him that I was thinking of staying either at the Plaza or the Waldorf, because they were famous hotels I had heard of growing up in Sacramento.

"Are you in your seventies?" he asked not unkindly. When he stopped chuckling he continued, "stay at the Royalton, trust me. It's more age appropriate."

The minute I walked in to the hotel I knew what he meant. The lobby was dimly lit and opened into a stylish lounge filled with hip young people dressed in black, chatting over exotic cocktails. It looked like a Calvin Klein underwear commercial. *Age* appropriate yes, but I doubted any of them were talking about the options market. Invisible to them in my grey slacks and blue blazer I checked in at the front desk and walked through the lobby carrying my UC Davis football duffel bag to take the elevator to my floor.

The hall was also dimly lit, stylish fixtures casting a soft yellow glow that made me feel welcomed. I found my room halfway down the hall and used my keycard to open the door. The bed was a one-foot thick futon mattress lying flat on the floor. I dropped my duffel bag and looked around the rest of the sparsely furnished but elegant room. Nothing about it said *finance* or felt very familiar but it was already late in New York so I unpacked and prepared for bed. Before lowering myself onto the futon, I looked out the window and saw the Algonquin hotel across the street. The Algonquin! Where Dorothy Parker had led the great round table, a literary "salon" nicknamed the "vicious circle" made up of some of the greatest critical thinkers of the 1920's: Robert Benchley, Edna Ferber, Noël Coward, Tallulah Bankhead, Harold Ross and Harpo Marx to name a few. The intelligent, witty and literary discourse of the vicious circle was well-known and beloved for bravely questioning the status quo. I lowered myself onto the futon wondering if I even knew what my status quo was.

I dozed off for a few brief spells but otherwise drifted through my thoughts. One minute thinking, *I am the master of the universe here to begin my climb to the top!* the next minute I'd panic, *What the hell am I doing here?* I wondered what I would say to the people I was meeting over the next five days. With my anxiety building in the stillness of the early morning, I got up from the futon, took a shower and ordered breakfast. When I sat down to eat, a sense of calm started to push away the anxiety. Whatever was going to happen would happen, I told myself. If the week went poorly, the worst that could happen was I would simply go back to trading Microsoft options. *At least I gave it a shot,* I thought to myself.

I learned a lot that week - starting with how hard it can be to get from midtown to downtown Manhattan on a Monday morning. Fortunately, I had left my room early planning on arriving in time to walk around the World Trade Center before my meeting at Shearson Lehman Brothers. As it turned out, traffic was terrible. I got to the building just in time to get through security and up to the Shearson Lehman offices on the 42nd floor by eighty-thirty.

My first meeting was with the man in charge of all the retail option business for Shearson. A man named Kevin Murphy. In trading, *retail business* comprises the smaller trades made buy non-professionals - a dentist selling five calls against a stock position or a housewife buying ten calls in a company that makes her favorite software. The bigger trades that come from institutions like hedge funds or banks are called *institutional business*. On the floor, institutional business is the meat and retail business, the gravy. We would rather trade with a retired accountant in Dubuque than a team of finance experts in Manhattan. At that time, Shearson was one of the largest providers of retail order flow.

Terry Brookshire and Kevin Murphy's boss, Dick Donsky, were old friends so Shearson was already routing their Micron order flow to the PSE; but with Terry leaving the floor and Donsky retiring there was no guarantee that this would continue. Kevin and I were a new generation, and though we didn't know it at the time, this meeting would begin a great business and personal relationship that would help both of our careers.

Kevin began the meeting by telling me they did not plan to make a change in their routing of Micron options unless there was a change in the level of service and liquidity. He was giving me a chance and my confidence surged back to 'master of the universe' level. The ball was in my court and I would take good care of it.

"Thank you, that's great," I told him. 'I'm confident you'll find that we continue the same level of service and liquidity."

With the sole purpose of the meeting accomplished, we went on to talk about our backgrounds and the options business in general. Kevin was only a few years older than me and, as it turns out, had wrestled in college. He was as focused on his career as I was on mine. I left the meeting feeling like I had not only secured the Shearson order flow but I'd also made a new friend. I was, however, wise enough to know other my New York meetings might not be as successful.

And they weren't.

One institutional trader told me that I had better hope they find a spotted owl under our trading floor or we would be extinct, adding:

"We don't need a stock exchange in 'Frisco.*"*

"Well," I managed to collect my thoughts enough to say, "if you become unhappy with Chicago and New York, maybe give San Francisco a try in Micron. We might surprise you."

I changed the topic to sports and soon learned we had both played football at Division II schools. He had gone to Lehigh University when they played Davis in a memorable national playoff game that ultimately eliminated my school. The game was played a few years before I got to Davis so we had not played against each other, but we laughed about the trials and tribulations of D2 football.

"I got to give you credit," he clapped me on the back as I was getting ready to leave, "we've never gotten a visit from a floor guy before. Not even the AMEX guys -- and they're right down the street!"

He turned to walk away and then stopped and faced me again.

"*If* I give you a shot you better not screw me," he said.

The results of the rest of my meetings were similar: customers already routing to the PSE agreed to continue if I continued to provide Terry's level of service, and customers that were routing to one of the other floors said they would likely never change their routing to San Francisco.

"Even if we were unhappy with the New York guys, we'd go to Chicago before San Fran," was the gist of it.

What was similar in all the meetings was a personal connection; I loved getting to know other people working in the options market. The majority of time in my meetings that week was spent asking questions: How did you come to work on an options desk? What is it like to work for a big firm? What do you do for excitement? All the people I met fascinated me: working in offices in tall towers, living in buildings with doormen or taking trains in from Long Island, taking clients to the best restaurants, front row tickets to incredible events. The people I met that week were the embodiment of the picture of success I formulated growing up in Sacramento.

Friday came and I had one morning meeting before taking a taxi to JFK airport. My body was exhausted but my mind felt charged. I collapsed into my seat on the plane and slept the whole way home.

Back on the floor on Monday, the crowd tortured me with stories of the good trades I missed. After the close, I gathered all of my receipts from the trip to give to my accountant. Tallying up the thousands of dollars I spent on the trip and thinking about the untold thousands more I would *surely* have made trading, I began to wonder if the trip was worth it. After all, I had little to show for it other than managing to keep the order flow I already had. The trip had been exciting and had certainly stroked my ego, but was it worth the cost?

It was.

The people I met on that trip became a network of industry connections that would serve me my entire career. Many of them rose through the ranks of their firms and in the industry just as my career progressed out west. Without the relationships I built on that and subsequent marketing visits to New York City, Boston, and Chicago I could not have accomplished nearly as much as I did. Case in point: after that first and pivotal week in Manhattan, I kept all of the order flow Terry had won and had even managed to convince a few of the others I had met in New York to make us their primary market. In fact, the trader who told me to hope we found a spotted owl under our floor ended up switching his order flow to me, a satisfying development to be sure.

Our share of the Micron volume rose to eighty-five percent. Garnering that much market share on the PSE in a battle against the AMEX *and* the CBOE was unprecedented. We had never even gotten a majority of the market in any issue that also traded on the industry leading CBOE, let alone both the CBOE and AMEX.

Micron was still a low volume tech stock that most people had never heard of so my unique accomplishment went mostly unnoticed. I was proud of what I had done, but I still made the majority of my profits trading Microsoft and winning a battle that nobody cares about is only so gratifying. Hiking on Mt. Tam one afternoon I dreamed about what would happen if Micron became more active. I pictured it trading enough volume to make it in to the top ten option volume lists. The higher I climbed up the mountain that day, the more active I imagined Micron. I pictured my crowd of ten to twelve market makers swollen to forty, surrounded by several floor brokers calling for markets. I pictured myself in the front of the crowd, directing the action and working the phones. I imagined myself on the board of governors - as Vice Chairman of the Board of Governors, just as Terry had been.

The next year, Micron became more active, finishing in the top ten options in the country. The busier it got, the more I dreamed and soon it became easier to visualize. The next year, Micron was the most active option stock in the U.S. markets and my pit grew to more than forty market makers, becoming the biggest pit on the PSE. The year after that, Micron traded more options in the first ten months than any other stock had ever traded in an entire year. From my dreamscape to reality: the most active option in the world was listed in San Francisco, Chicago, and New York, but the volume traded in San Francisco and I was the reason.

*   *   *

The guarantees I made to my customers were more than the exchange requires of its members so I needed to coerce my crowd to cooperate with me in servicing the order flow. I made an implicit deal (well, usually implicit -- unfortunately, some people needed things spelled out for them) with the market makers in my crowd: We are all in this together and playing by my rules is the best way for all of us to prosper.

And prosper we did. Volume drives profit, and we could hardly keep up with ours. Most of the market makers understood the implicit deal, others needed it spelled out for them but ultimately fell in line. Knowing that a good crowd can be a specialist's biggest asset, I tried to run my crowd like Solomon the Wise. The market makers recognized my efforts to secure the order flow and were happy to do their part to service it. There were, however, other exchange members who were critical of my methods and thought I was getting too much for my role as Lead Market Maker (LMM) – I was guaranteed fifty percent of the options that traded on my markets. These members knew little about my marketing trips or the sacrifices (read: lost money) I made every day to keep my customers coming back. Even when the crowd helped me fill a "bad" trade, I traded (at least) my usual half.

One member in particular, a Russian-American Libertarian Jew from Minnesota named Jacob Tsyros, considered me a threat. Tsyros wasn't the kind of enemy who confronted or dared show his dislike. Instead, he attacked through gossip and innuendo, false accusations, and second- or third-party interference.

One Monday I arrived in my pit to find a new member wearing a temporary badge, gathering with the usual members of the crowd. There was nothing unusual about this, every newbie wanted to trade in the most active pit on the floor. What would have been unusual was if he lasted. I wouldn't have given him a second thought except, a few minutes before the opening bell, I saw him slip to the back of the crowd to confer with, of all people, Jacob Tsyros.

When the opening bell rang I turned to trade the opening rotation. Standing at the front of the crowd next to my friend and lead broker Jamie Cottrell, I gave my markets as the exchange official called for them while Jamie represented his orders. At the first pause in both of our responsibilities, I pulled Jamie aside.

"Who's the new guy?" I asked.

"Don't know," Jamie said, looking at me suspiciously. He wasn't accustomed to me noticing a new market maker. "Why do you care?"

"I saw him talking to *Jaaake* before the opening," I said, referring to Tsyros by his Minnesota-accented nickname.

"I'll find out," he said.

Jamie was a great lieutenant: he was my cajoler, enforcer, explainer, friend, psychiatrist and spy. A six-foot-five American Irishman with a big personality, an Irish temper, and a huge heart, Jamie was the best broker on the floor. He lived out loud and knew everybody on the floor and soon he knew everything about our new crowd member.

"His name is Larry Christianson," Jamie told me a few hours later. "His older brother is Jake's best friend. He stood in the Genentech pit behind Tsyros all last week like some kind of disciple. Now he's on a seat with a Jake's money and a week on the floor."

The connection between Christianson and Tsyros concerned me although I didn't expect to hear much from him for a few months. New members barely speak to other market makers for the first month (beyond what is required to conduct business), and then only guardedly for a long while after that. Most of them didn't last long enough to get that point. Veteran crowd members knew not to get attached to newbie's until they survived six months and proved themselves capable. So it was not surprising that Christianson hardly said a word for the first few days, though I did notice he was conferring with Tsyros a lot more than might normally be expected. On the third day, Christianson show his intentions.

At the beginning of the trading day, all orders with small volume are automatically matched with market makers and traded electronically. These are the simplest retail customers, unsophisticated and trading less than ten options at a time. They sold on the bid and paid the offer and we made a lot of money trading with them. I always want these customers to have a good experience and make money for retention reasons: happy customers come back with more and bigger trades. An option trade is not a zero-sum outcome; both sides can be profitable on the same trade. Unlike most customers, market makers actively trade stock to manage option positions; and if correctly executed, the money lost to the customer on the option was less than the trader's profit in the stock.

Exchange rules state that an electronic trade is always a "good" trade - meaning it can't be broken after it trades unless both parties agree - because computers theoretically cannot miscommunicate so whatever trade you receive has to be what you ordered. Errors do happen from time to time – usually a keypunch error by a trader on a retail desk (often the same trader who decides where to route their order flow) -- and most market makers will allow the trade to be "busted" when a retail customer asks. Of course, almost all the errors we hear about are losing trades, but we *bust* them as professional courtesies.

That Wednesday, when the opening rush died down, I noticed the woman who ran the automated business (or, "the wire") waiting to speak to me outside earshot of my trading crowd. Liz Alvarez ran the wire for Kevin Murphy at Shearson.

"Hey, Liz," I greeted her. "What's up?"

Liz and I had a good working relationship built on our shared respect for Kevin and developed through conversations like the one we were about to have.

"Sorry to bother you with this," she said, "but I had ten-lot error from the opening and the trader who did a one-lot won't bust it. The other nine are already out of the system but I don't want to tell Kevin he has a one-lot error."

"He doesn't," I said. "I'll take the trade."

This meant I would sell one option at a losing price to one of my competitors, basically writing him a check.

"Thanks for telling me," I paused before leaving. "By the way, who won't bust it?"

"Some new guy, L52," Liz said. "Clears FOC. You want to talk to him before we process the trade?"

"No," I told her.

An intense but calm anger rose in my chest.

L52 was Larry Christianson's acronym. I knew Jake sent this guy into my crowd to make money, but now I realized he also intended for him to be a wrench in the works of my operation. I checked my anger and tried giving them the benefit of the doubt: after all, it was just a one-lot trade on Christianson's third day. Maybe he didn't understand the implicit rules of the pit yet.

I knew time would reveal his true intentions.

In the end, it didn't even take that long.

Christianson soon began to obstruct anything he could. He had an annoying personality and seemed to be without shame so he was very good at his role as obstructionist. He was the worst type of citizen: taking advantage of every benefit but refusing to pay the fees. A poacher. My anger intensified until I couldn't think of anything other than this struggle with Christianson. It felt more than personal. In a finely balanced system like a trading pit, one bad actor can ruin the agreed-upon order. I call it the *lowest common denominator* effect. No doubt we have all experienced it many times.

You are waiting to get off the freeway in an "exit only" lane that is backed up a quarter of a mile and moving slowly. While you wait, car after car speeds past on your left, cutting ahead of the line just in time to make the exit. As a result, your lane has come to a stop. Pretty soon cars that were behind you change lanes, speed past you and cut back into the front of line. They are following examples set by the line-cutters. Together they become the *lowest common denominator*. Do you follow suit and change lanes? How about the next time you are at the exit in the same situation, do you wait to change into the exit lane closer to the exit?

My anger intensified by the fear that Christianson would be the lowest common denominator that would drag down the delicate order I had taken great pains to establish. I could think of nothing but destroying this threat, this Larry Christianson, and vowed to do it even if it cost me money. With my rights as a specialist, my trading experience, and my superior capitalization I knew I could make his job very difficult and doing so became my top priority. I went after every one of his trades, selling what he bought and buying what he sold to push the prices against him.

And I lost money every day.

A lot of money. To Christianson. It was driving me insane. After a particularly bad day, I headed to Mt. Tam to sort out my mind on a hike to the top. About fifteen minutes into my climb, I felt a cloud lift from overhead when, almost in an instant, I could see the situation I had on my hands. I realized I was being a fool. Jake's intention was to disrupt my business, but there I was doing it for him.
The solution was simple and within my power: all I had to do was stop.

So that's what I did. I stopped.

I told myself the little injustices Christianson inflicted on my crowd were the cost of doing business. I forced myself to ignore him in the pit and soon I genuinely didn't notice him enough to ignore him.

In trading, if you're standing in a pit, you're spending seven and a half hours with the people around you. You come to learn there are many ways you can screw them but just as important a lesson to learn is understanding that they, too, have many ways to screw you right back, these people standing alongside you every single day. That's why competitors will help each other out in small ways whenever they can -- there are great benefits for community members who recognize and live up to their responsibilities.

Sure enough, when I left Christianson alone, the crowd schooled him in the laws of our fiefdom. Devoid of the bias I knew I had, the crowd assumed Larry Christianson was a naïve new citizen and, with peer pressure and eagle-eyed market makers, he fell in line. The writing was on the wall for Larry anyway: none of his obstruction tactics had worked and on top of that he'd been losing capital so Christianson must have known his allegiance to Tsyros was starting to cost him money. Larry was a lot of things -- loud, obnoxious and annoying -- but he wasn't stupid.

Quietly and with little fanfare, Larry Christianson capitulated to my unwritten rules of conduct in the pit and order was restored both literally and figuratively. Everyone towed the line and no more tight fists of anger in my chest. Larry Christianson lasted a few years and the crowd accepted him like he was it's crazy little brother: annoying but ultimately harmless.

I almost started to like him.

Wise Speech

"And what is called right speech? Abstaining from lying, from divisive speech, from abusive speech, and from gossip...a statement endowed with five factors is well spoken, not ill spoken. Which five? It is spoken at the right time. It is spoken in truth. It is spoken affectionately. It is spoken beneficially. It is spoken with a mind of goodwill."

Okay, I know what you're thinking: how can the banter, aggression, and abuse thrown around the floor be *wise speech*? It is one the first questions people ask whenever I discuss Buddhism and trading. I also know that some of my colleagues and competitors from the floor will laugh out loud when they hear that I have written a book about using Buddhism to create a peaceful and satisfying career and life. One in particular, a broker who was in my pit intermittently every day, will be incredulous. I know this because his daughter is one of my daughter's best friends, and he has been crystal clear about his feelings towards me. Years after we worked together, I ran into him at a local coffee shop and he looked like he was seeing Hitler. He left without getting a coffee.

Tim Dutton [not his real name] was a floor broker representing professional customers, our competitors among them, including market makers in the Micron pits in Chicago and New York. He would always arrive in a flash, yelling what he wanted to do, knowing that if we saw him coming we would try to beat him to whatever his customers wanted to trade. They traded like we did and when they sent an order to our floor it was because we had missed something so we were either forced by exchange rules to make a losing trade to honor a 'bad' market, or we would miss out on a profitable trade with a customer order that we had overlooked. And what was worse - our loss was our competitor's gain, which was infuriating. Tim had a tough job.

On a trading floor tempers flare on a daily sometimes hourly basis and there are few restrictions on speech. Vicious insults are spoken as quickly as they are forgotten and abuse is heaped on anyone who shows that it bothers them. I unleashed tirades on all sorts of people, but Tim received the worst of them. There were other brokers representing similar customers, but Tim drew the bulk of my ire. Neatly dressed and fastidious, Tim combed his hair conservatively and sprayed it neatly in place. He looked more like the pharmaceutical salesman he would become many years later than the floor trader he was trying hard to be back then. He had an artificial sheen to him that was discordant with everything I loved about the trading floor.

Tim worked for a company that specialized in professional business so we treated him as an adversary from the start, talking with disdain and heaping insults on him. Although Tim got it a little worse, every new trader is abused on the floor – it is a rite of passage. The only way to stop it is to pretend it doesn't bother you. It bothered Tim, and it showed. I don't think he had ever been cast as a villain before and he wasn't sure how to handle it. First, he tried a friendly appeal.

"Hey guys," he'd almost cajole the crowd. "I'm just doin' my job here."

He dropped his g's and said 'gotta' and 'gonna' in an effort to sound like a-man-of-the-people but it sounded as contrived as it was.

"Everyone's gotta make a livin'," Tim would shrug. "These guys are gonna trade through somebody, gimme a break."

It was the same argument I had once used to justify my work impounding student's bicycles for rent money in college, but I wasn't buying it from Tim.

"If selling my soul were the only way I could work down here, I'd find another place to work," I said. "Do you care that everyone you work with thinks you're a bottom-feeding parasite? I know I couldn't live with that."

Realizing he wasn't going to get an ounce of sympathy, Tim became adversarial.

"Do a better job making markets and you won't see me," he said to me. "If the CBOE guys weren't better than you guys, I'd be out of a job. I don't want to have to walk out here and pick you off all the time."

This went over like a donut joke in a police station. The entire crowd turned on him and he became a verbal punching bag. I said things to him I wish I had not; things that were far off the Eightfold Noble Path. I hope I would behave differently were I in the same situation now, but at the time I used some very *un*wise speech. In retrospect I can see that the venom in my words was only infecting me. There is a line between banter and abuse and it's an important one not to cross; but because I didn't like the way he looked or the job he did, and because a vitriolic crowd encouraged me, I crossed it with Tim. And stayed across it.

My abuse may have taken a toll on Tim but what I didn't realize until later was that it took an even bigger toll on me. The energy and thought that went into battling with Tim had distracted me from more profitable pursuits, the venom of anger infected my every thought. It was like letting a rude stewardess ruin your whole vacation.

This is why it's called a Buddhist *practice*; we strive to be wise but sometimes we are not. We need to keep *practicing*. There is always room for development. Constantly working to stay on the path is important but learning from our deviations from the path is the real work. We don't find a path to make a camp there; we find it so we can continue our journey.

*   *   *

The systems, rules, rates, and customer service the exchange provided were the foundation upon which I built my business. The Pacific Stock Exchange was a membership organization, which means each seat gives its owner both the right to trade on the floor and an ownership share in the exchange. Members owned and governed the exchange like shareholders do a corporation. And like shareholders, members vote on important issues and elect a board of governors to represent them. The board hires a CEO, who then builds an executive team and staff to operate the daily business of running an exchange. The board of governors consisted of six floor members, six off-floor industry members, and twelve public governors from outside the financial industry.

Serving the board were several member committees that governed trading on each of the floors. The committee members had to be active on the appropriate floor and were chosen by their peers. The most important committee was the Options Floor Trading Committee (OFTC), which made all the rules that governed trading and behavior on the options floor. On everything from the dress code - which was openly flouted and difficult to enforce - to the rules governing how a trade is executed, the committee made and enforced the laws, almost like a combination of Congress and the FBI. Each member of the OFTC is a "Floor Official" and is responsible for settling any disputes that arise in the pits they are assigned to officiate. Never an easy job.

I was nominated to the OFTC in my third year of trading. My business was growing rapidly and I had become vocal about the issues facing the market making community, which were mostly technological. The more progressive members supported my candidacy and ensured my nomination. Computers were rapidly changing the competitive environment and I knew that the exchange needed to change in order to survive. However, members who had made a good living in a certain way, under a certain system, for many years, were resistant to changing *anything.* The OFTC consisted of six market makers and six floor brokers and was known to be very contentious. At the age of twenty-four, I looked the part of fresh-faced upstart, and the conservative members marked me as an enemy before my first meeting.

Walking into the exchange conference room for my first meeting, I could feel tension in the room as the members chose their seats around the table. I tried to discern a pattern in their choices and wondered where to sit, ultimately deciding on an empty seat at the far end of the table between two other empty seats.

As the rest of the committee members arrived for the meeting, two members I hardly knew filled the seats next to me. The Chairman opened the meeting by introducing new members, beginning with me. He caught me by surprise, though, when he asked me to say a few words about myself. My plan had been to observe a few meetings before saying anything, and I was not prepared. I sputtered through some generic remarks and sat back down.

After the rest of the introductions, the committee turned to the first order of business, a simple rule change that had been proposed by exchange staff to expedite operations. The rule change would allow the exchange to automate the smallest trades, which our technology was programmed to do but our current rules did not allow. After the exchange attorney explained the proposed rule, he asked the committee for questions or comments. There were none. Around the table the committee members shook their heads or sat quietly. I wasn't surprised because it seemed like an easy decision: our competitors had already automated these trades and three firms were threatening to leave if we didn't follow suit. The attorney left the room to allow the committee to deliberate the rule change.

The chairman opened the meeting for discussion. The committee members sat quietly, shuffling their papers and looking down. Finally, after a long silence, an older member, an Italian floor broker named John Cappiello, raised his hand.

Cappy, as he was known, was the prototypical floor broker: grumpy but efficient, uncompromising but fair, unwilling to take crap from anybody but underneath it all, a pushover with a big heart. The Chairman nodded for him to proceed. Cappy started with vague comments about the nefarious intentions of the Exchange staff, then further digressed into a long story that appeared to be unrelated to the issue up for vote. He finished with a paranoid rant about the staff wanting to get rid of him, personally -- a stretch that would tear the arm off a Stretch Armstrong. Furthermore, it was exasperating: Cappy was making general arguments against seismic changes in the industry that were happening whether we wanted them to or not and yes, automation was killing jobs everywhere but we were meant to be discussing the specific rule change. I thought I could help focus the dialog.

"I don't understand what all that has to do with the issue at hand," I said.

My comment had the opposite effect of what I intended.

All six of the floor brokers started talking at once. Many were saying I had just proven everything Cappy had said was right and some were claiming the market makers were conspiring to run the floor unabated. The chairman, a floor broker, did nothing to stop or even slow the cacophony of conspiracy theories. I wanted to interrupt and explain my comment, but I knew I could only do further damage so I remained silent.

The floor brokers were upset because they currently handled these small orders and charged a per-contract commission. The rule change meant they would lose some revenue, but small orders were only one small part of their business. An automatic execution is instantaneous, a manual one takes minutes – a floor broker has to receive the order from a runner, trade the options, and send the report back to his desk where it is entered into the firm's system and transmitted to the customer. The floor brokers were right that their jobs were being threatened - like many others in the last quarter century - by computers that could do their job faster, better and cheaper. It's a struggle that reaches back to the story of John Henry trying to beat a steam engine driving railroad stakes with his hammer and shaker. But progress rolls on with its own force. Humans must adapt or get out of the way. John Henry did neither; he won the race with the steam engine but dropped dead at the finish line.

John Henry said to the Captain,
You can bring your steam drill around
You can bring your steam drill out on the job,
I'll beat your steam drill down, down, down,
Beat your steam drill down

Now his shaker said to John Henry,
Man ain't nothing but a man.

But before I'd let that steam drill beat me down,

I'd die with a hammer in my hand.

They took John Henry to the graveyard,

Laid him down in the sand.

Every locomotive comes a-rollin' by

Hollered, there lies a steel driving man, oh Lord

There lies a steel driving man

I am not saying the floor brokers were wrong. In fact, over the next decade computers would replace about ninety percent of them. But when faced with a choice like John Henry's, the brokers who survived and prospered were the ones who embraced the electronic environment. The rest -- the majority -- left the options floor by the early 2000s. Many of them went on to become mortgage brokers.

All that aside, the issue we were debating was simple: we had three major customers threatening to reroute *all* of their order flow – not just the small orders - to a more automated exchange if we didn't make the electronic changes. Either the floor brokers would lose ten percent of these firms' business or we would all lose one hundred percent.

 The debate roiled on for another hour, often going in circles. Every floor broker on the committee spoke of elaborate sacrifices this change would force them to make and argued it was the first step on the proverbial slippery slope that ultimately landed in unemployment and homelessness. Wives and children were referenced and the rhetoric soared. Of course, to some degree they were right, but it was like being a passenger on the Titanic yelling, "I don't care if it's sinking, I'm having a great cruise and I'm not leaving!"

After two hours of vitriolic debate, the fever in the room broke and there was quiet. Matt Adams, a senior market maker on the committee, slowly raised his hand to be recognized to speak - a formality that had been discarded for the previous hour of debate. The chairman recognized him.

"I know this is a tough thing for all of us to accept," Matt said. "And I hear the frustration from our floor brokers who will make the first sacrifice. Cappy, when you say this will affect your bottom line, and therefore your family, I know you're speaking the truth. And it's a hard truth. You all have worked hard to build your businesses and this is a hit you shouldn't have to take. I know it's easy for me to say but I don't think there is anything else we can do. What would happen to you if these firms pulled *all* of their business?"

Matt let the question hang in a moment of silence. Some of the floor brokers were looking down but all of them were nodding.

"If that's all the discussion, do I have a motion?" asked the chairman, eager to reach a resolution.

A motion was made and seconded.

The resolution passed.

*　　　　　*　　　　　*

In my abbreviated college career, the most valuable class I took was called Philosophy of Language and Communication. In it, we learned there are dozens of ways in which we communicate with one another: words, inflections, sounds, gestures, and facial expressions, to name a few. We learned about nuance and how a single sentence can have a number of completely different meanings depending on how it is spoken.

"Great, I got the only lean piece of the roast," could be said with either excitement or sarcasm – both indicate opposite things. Without being conscious of it, we employ some of these devices or *cues* every time we communicate. And though we should, we don't usually listen intently enough to detect and decipher all of these cues. My professor's rather pessimistic conclusion was that because our listening is flawed, most human communication is largely misunderstood.

Sometimes, it's in fairly harmless ways: when I hear *great! I got the only lean piece of the roast* I might think you love lean meat when in reality you loved fatter cuts.

In trading, words have financial consequences so communication must be perfect. There is a specific jargon for everything on the floor and all traders must learn it. When you are a *buyer* you make a *bid*, and when bidding, you bid *for;* when you are a *seller,* you make an *offer*, and when offering you offer *at.* I still chafe when I hear someone say "I made an offer to buy a house" or "I'd sell you my ticket for one hundred dollars." These are not grammatically incorrect, but on the floor, precision is required so we made our own usage rules. The language of the floor has power. If you say, "I'll bid a dollar for a hundred" and someone says "sold" you bought a hundred for a dollar.

Managing traders also requires precise communication, especially when it pertains to annual bonus compensation. Market makers are paid a very small monthly salary with most of their compensation coming in an annual bonus at the end of the year. When fifty to ninety-five percent of your take-home pay comes annually, you learn to listen for any clues as to what that number will be. As a manager, it was my job to guide trader's compensation expectations throughout the year. I never wanted to surprise a trader with their check, even pleasantly. I learned quickly there was a certain way to communicate this guidance.

The first thing I learned is that all nuance is lost in financial conversations.

All of it.

Only the numbers matter; all the other ways we communicate are lost or cherry-picked to support the listener's conclusion. And that conclusion will always be the most favorable possible for the listener. So, I could say:

"Based on your performance to date, the expected range of your bonus is two hundred to two hundred and twenty-five thousand."

I could even explain that, "if the year finishes strongly for you and for the firm it could be two hundred and fifty, maybe even more if everything goes perfectly. But, as you know, if your performance *declines* or if the firm has an unexpected loss, your bonus could be lower or you could receive nothing."

But all the trader hears is:

"Your bonus will be at least two hundred and fifty thousand. Probably more."

This is human nature. When we are shopping for a car and we are told the model we want sells for thirty-five to forty thousand dollars, we think we should get it for thirty-four.

I also learned that when communicating important information, it is best to use the fewest words possible; likewise, and perhaps more importantly, the fewer numbers used, the better. When traders pressed for specificity, I learned to react like a political pundit repeating the same talking point to every question.

In any discussion, numbers take on a life of their own once you speak them. The ones that grow in stature are the ones the listener wants to hear so by the time the year ends, if expectations are not kept in check, the trader may come to expect an outcome that was a long shot at best. So, the simpler the declarative sentence, the better:

"Based on current performance and variable to your and the firm's performance for the rest of the year, you should expect a bonus between two hundred and two hundred and twenty-five thousand dollars."

Wise Conduct

"Refrain from taking what is not freely given.
Refrain from coveting other's possessions and positions, and from resenting their good
fortune. Resentment of other's good fortune becomes a wall that prevents you from
improving your own fortunes. Refrain from [misuse of] intoxicants."

Not long after my first marketing trip to NYC, I arrived in my crowd before the opening and found John George, who ran Morgan Stanley's brokerage operation on the PSE, waiting to speak with me.

"Hey kid, can I talk to you for a second?"

"Sure," I said, following John to his desk in the Morgan Stanley booth which was adjacent to ours.

"One of my traders wants to talk to you," John said. "His name is Mark Neuberger. He's a *goodguy*."

In the markets *goodguy* is spoken like a single word and means someone with integrity.

"I don't know what it's about," he added, in answer to my puzzled expression.

Morgan Stanley had a large, well-capitalized and profitable options trading desk to service their customers and were known to dislike trading on exchange floors. When I visited Morgan's New York offices on my first marketing trip, I met with a man named Andy Brenner who appeared to view me as a competitor and waved me off, saying that Morgan "didn't need anything" from me.

"We ask no quarter and give no quarter," Brenner had said with complete sincerity.

John punched a flashing button and handed me his phone, gesturing for me to start talking.

"This is Rob Kovell," I said into the phone.

"Hey Rob, Mark Neuberger. Andy Brenner said I should give you a call. How are you doing?"

"I'm well, thanks," I said wary of what could come from Andy Brenner.

Mark got right down to business:

"I have several large players in Micron that are going to be active moving *size*," Mark said. In trading *size* means big. "I need a floor to get it on the tape and Andy told me to try you. I will bring blocks of five or ten thousand options and, of course, want to trade them myself, but I'd be willing to work with you."

"Well, I am a thousand up on everything and the crowd is usually about the same," I told him. "We usually ask for half of the first five thousand contracts and the rest is yours."

"That seems fair. I'll make sure Johnny lets you know when it's me," he said, referring to his broker.

"Great Mark, thanks for the call," I said. "I look forward to doing business with you."

What I didn't know at the time was that Mark had devised a strategy that Morgan's investment bank pitched to the large personal computer (PC) makers. Micron's main product is a simple memory chip called a DRAM chip which, because of its simplicity, trades like a commodity. In other words, they are what they are and price is driven by supply and demand, not product improvement and upgrade cycles.

When Mark called me, DRAM prices were skyrocketing and demand for them was at an all-time high. Explosive growth in the PC market combined with rapidly expanding processor speed – the bigger processors required more memory per machine – had caused a shortage in supply which doubled the price-per-chip. Micron couldn't raise production fast enough to keep up with demand so they increased prices driving a three-hundred percent rise in their share price. Companies like Dell bought massive amounts of DRAM chips to include in their machines and competition in the PC market made it difficult to pass the increasing expense to the consumer so their margins were taking a beating.

Mark's idea was for them buy *call options* in Micron to hedge their risk in memory chip cost. If DRAM prices continued to rise, so would Micron stock and the value of the call options and the profit on the trade would offset the increased cost. If DRAM prices decreased, the savings in acquisition cost would make the cost of the options insignificant. It's like an insurance policy, best if you never get your money back.

The idea was brilliant and soon most of the computer manufacturers were using Micron options to hedge the risk of the volatile DRAM market. Mark had not exaggerated; he regularly entered orders to buy five or ten thousand call options at a time. Call buyers are a valuable find: the most popular options strategy is the *covered write* - selling out of the money calls against a long stock position – so liquidity providers like us always have a call inventory to sell. Mark and I split the trades amicably, worked well together and ultimately became close friends. When I was vice chairman, I recruited him to join me on the PSE Board where he became an invaluable ally and a productive governor. I would never have dreamed any of this possible when I left my meeting with Andy Brenner and I was glad I hadn't said what had been on my mind or I don't think I would have gotten the business.

My Micron position and profits, for the first time ever, were my largest. Microsoft had always been my golden goose; I had made my career trading it and I thought I would never stop. But with the added volume from Mark, our Micron market share topped seventy-five percent, an important level. Fidelity Investments was the last major retail order flow provider who did not send route their order flow to the Pacific. They had their own brokerage staff on the CBOE so it was cheaper for them to send their business there. I had spoken with them several times and they had said they would only consider switching if our market share was consistently above seventy-five percent. I called every week our market share stayed above their threshold and sent them a volume report and, after three months, they finally capitulated. It was the only time Fidelity ever chose the PSE over the CBOE and I still have a copy of the first order they sent us hanging in my office.

With the Fidelity business our market share was in the mid-eighties and I became so busy in Micron that entire days went by without me making any trades in Microsoft. When the exchange approached me insisting we split Micron from the Microsoft pit and create a new post I barely resisted, even though this meant I would no longer able to make markets in Microsoft options. It marked the end of an era for me but I hardly had time to recognize it; Micron had become the most active stock on the PSE.

I was overwhelmed and needed help. I hired two exchange staff to help my clerk keep up with my trading activity; their most important asset was they could start immediately. We were barely able to stay afloat in the raging volume, and the trading was so difficult and steady that I began to slur my words in the afternoons without having had a single drink. I wouldn't have believed I would ever get to the point that I was hoping for a *slow* day, but there I was, praying for a break in the action.

Then one day, a Shearson broker came in asking for a market good for a thousand contracts -- a new customer was interested in trading Micron options. Though we didn't know it yet, this customer would become a great whale for us. We called him "MT" because the account number on his Shearson orders started with those letters. That first day, I bought three thousand Micron call options. Over the next few days, the stock and the calls MT bought, rallied sharply. When the Shearson broker came in to quote the market for MT a week later we smiled and thought - nice trade, the options had tripled in value and we assumed he would sell them a take his three-hundred percent return. But when the broker came back he had an order to *buy* fifteen hundred more. We sold those on the offer and scrambled to buy stock to hedge. As the melee to hedge roared on, MT came back to buy another three thousand. By the time all the orders were filled and my positions hedged I felt like I had run an ironman triathlon. When the closing bell rang I sat down among the day's detritus, where I had been standing all day.

The rally continued and the options doubled again. When MT's broker asked for a market we had no idea if he would buy more or take his profit. We knew he owned four thousand options. We also knew the options had gone up so much that the amount of stock we needed to sell when we bought them back was twice as much as the initial trade. As the stock had moved up we adjusted our positions by buying more stock against the calls to keep our portfolios profitable. Now we would need to sell it all quickly.

When the Shearson broker returned, I could tell from his demeanor he had something big.

"Jan 55 Micron," he was confirming our market and sizes were still the same. "Is my quoted market still good?"

I checked the underlying stock and the market.

"No change," I said, speaking for the crowd.

"I'll sell you the two thousand you showed," he said.

The crowd erupted in a frenzy of hedging.

"How are they now?" the broker asked me while holding out the market order so I could see it.

The order was for six thousand contracts, and the price limit was crossed out. This market order had to be filled as quickly as possible at the best price available. We filled the order and adjusted our positions and we moved over two billion dollars in assets in less than five minutes.

MT had sold out the options he owned and sold two thousand more short, now betting the stock would go back down. It did and the calls expired worthless. It was a master class in call trading. I couldn't figure out what this customer was - he traded like an institution, but his orders came through Shearson's retail desk. I had a marketing trip to New York planned and looked forward to discussing MT with my friend at Shearson, Kevin Murphy.

When I arrived in their office, Kevin thanked me for taking such good care of their new customer.

"Happy to do it," I replied. "Thanks for the opportunity."

I couldn't help myself, I had to find out more about MT.

"Who is this guy?" I asked. "I've never seen anyone trade like him."

"Let's talk to Craig," Kevin said, gesturing to one of his colleagues that I had met on a previous trip. "He's the one who handles the account."

"Hey Craig, good to see you," I said as we shook hands and clapped backs. "Thanks for the business. This guy sure throws some risk around!"

"Yeah, he's...*unique*," Craig said, choosing his words carefully. "When he calls me with orders you'd think they were five lots, he's so calm."

"Wow," I said. "Interesting. You know anything else about him?"

"He says he made money investing in tech startups, but he's vague about it. Compliance is still on him for more documentation."

"How'd you guys find him?" I asked.

"He walked into our midtown branch with a check and said he wanted to trade options," Craig said. "The local almost fainted when he saw the amount."

"Well, the way he's been trading, he's got a bigger check coming back," I said with a laugh.

Over the next few months MT continued trading bigger and bigger and was soon regularly trading five thousand options at a time. He was less successful though; buying large numbers of options, and then doubling down, before watching them expire worthless. The more he lost the more active he became, trading several times a day trying to capture small moves in the market. A difficult game when you are paying retail commissions.

One morning I arrived in the crowd at six-fifteen in the morning, as usual. The Shearson clerk was waiting for me and told me Kevin Murphy wanted to talk to me. I followed him back to their booth and he called Kevin and handed me the phone.

"Hey, Kevin," I said. "What's up?"

"Hey, Rob. Im going to have Craig pick up too," he said and after saying something off the line, Craig joined us.

"We wanted to let you know we closed the MT account yesterday," he began. "The customer refused to provide the required documentation on the source of his funds and compliance shut down the account."

"I'm sorry to hear that," I said. "It's been a lot of fun working with you guys on these orders."

"We think he will just go somewhere else," Craig said. "If you happen to notice where, would you mind letting us know?"

Later that same day, a Prudential broker started quoting and trading Micron in large numbers. It was obviously MT. I called Kevin and told him who was handling the account and he thanked me. I could hear the disappointment in his voice over losing such a large account to a competitor.

A few weeks later, I woke up on a Monday morning feeling sick. I had a fever, felt weak and I almost threw up in the shower but, with MT around, I knew I had to get to work. I drank some water, ate half a dry bagel and felt a little better. I got to the floor still feeling clammy and a little weak but I put it aside to get ready for the day's onslaught.

Right after the opening, the Prudential broker asked for a market in a combo - selling deep expensive puts and buying at the money calls. It was a huge bet on the rally continuing and I would need to buy more than one hundred thousand shares for every thousand combos I traded. I told the broker the price where we would do the trade a thousand times.

"Done," he said. "I can do that ten thousand times."

I almost fainted, and not from the fever. MT wanted to buy the option equivalent of a million shares of Micron. I traded a thousand combos with him and told my stock trader to sell two hundred thousand shares of Micron. He dropped the sports page he had been reading looked down at his computer, then up at me with shock and confusion.

"It only takes orders up to ninety-nine thousand," he said.

"Then sell ninety-nine thousand twice!" I yelled.

My clerk quickly went to work on his handheld stock execution terminal, but before he got any response on the first two orders, the Prudential broker said,

"How are they after?"

Meaning at what price would we trade more.

"A quarter away for another two grand," I said.

"Done," he said. "And after?"

I was now longer than I had ever been -- if the stock fell quickly I could lose everything. I stared at Johnny, my stock clerk, but he shrugged to indicate the machine had not responded to our orders. I was long more than four hundred thousand in Micron, four times more than I ever had been.

I told Johnny to sell another ninety-nine thousand.

"Give me a minute," I said to the broker.

"I've got a market order here, what is the market on seven thousand more?" he yelled. "What's the market?"

I put my arm around his shoulder, and in a very calm tone said,

"You see that kid over there?" I pointed at my stock clerk. "Until he tells me I have sold my first two hundred grand, there is no market. You do understand the amount of risk this requires? Work with me and we will get it done."

I had forgotten about my fever and the adrenaline from the risk outweighed my exhaustion. We filled that order in the next five minutes as my stock hedges were put in place. When I was done, my illness returned stronger than it had been and I suddenly felt dizzy. I wanted to go lie down on my office but was too afraid to leave the floor in case MT wasn't done.

And he wasn't.

Two hours later he came back to trade out of that position for a very small gain. Twenty minutes later he came back again to open another ten-thousand contract position. I traded more contracts in that one day with him than I usually did in two weeks. Throughout the day he made several massive short-term bets but I was able to stay just ahead of him and had a very good day. He did not.

In fact, he lost several hundred thousand dollars.

When the closing bell rang I felt like I had run a triathlon and then played middle linebacker in an NFL game. I sank to the floor and leaned against the wall, unable to believe all that had happened. When I regained enough energy to stand up, I gave my trading coat to Johnny and went straight to my car to drive home. I was so hot I sweated through my shirt and even my tie was soaking wet by the time I got home. I fell straight into bed and didn't wake up until three o'clock the following morning.

I woke in a pool of sweat but I could tell I no longer had a fever. I felt like I needed to drink a pool full of water, though, and my stomach was growling. I remembered I hadn't eaten anything the day before and got out of bed, grabbed my robe, went to the kitchen, and cooked a big breakfast. One of a very few times I was up early enough to enjoy breakfast at home. I felt my strength returning with every bite.

When I arrived in the pit that morning the Prudential broker was waiting for me.

"Sam Terner needs to speak to you," he said.

Sam was on the board of governors and ran the options department at Prudential. I went back to their booth and picked up the phone.

"Hey, Sam," I said. "How are you?"

"Well, it's a strange morning around here Robbie, I can tell you that," he replied.

"What's going on?"

"The FBI showed up at seven to seize all the records related to our new customer," Sam said. "What do you know about this guy?"

"Nothing really," I answered. "Just that Shearson had trouble with him and closed the account."

"How long they have him?" he asked.

"The last six months or so. Crazy volume, not quite like yesterday, but still huge."

"Great they get all the commissions and we end up with the bad press," Sam said. "Whatever this guy is, it's rotten."

I told Sam I was sorry to hear it, and I was; I had made lot of money trading with MT and was sorry to see him go. He never made another trade and I wondered who the hell he had been.

A few years later, I was watching *60 Minutes* and was surprised to see the lead story was about an option trading fraud.

It was MT!

His name was Edward J. Reiners. Mr. Reiners had been a mid-level executive at Philip Morris for ten years but left to start a video rental store in New Jersey. From the back room of the video store, Mr. Reiners talked a consortium of banks into loaning him three hundred and twenty-three million dollars. Posing as a Philip Morris employee, Reiners told the bank he was working on a secret project called "Project Star" that was set up to find new revenue streams because the company worried about anti-smoking campaign eroding their core business. Reiners told the bank that they needed ultra-secrecy because they were afraid the project would spook their employees and investors. He told them it needed to stay off of the corporate finances in order to stay secret, so the company had set up a separate LLC to fund Project Star. But more amazingly, he told the bankers that the project was so secret that they were not to contact anyone else at Philip Morris about it. Whatever came up, they were to call him directly and he would handle it. The bankers agreed and wired the money to the LLC controlled by Reiners. It was a check from this LLC that he had brought to the midtown branch of Shearson when he opened his account.

Reiners could have just run with the money at this point, but he would have become a fugitive. He had the perfect crime in mind. Reiners planned to trade with the money until he doubled it, then pay back the original amount and be left with more than three-hundred million dollars. In his mind, once he paid back the loan there would be no reason to investigate his story so he would be free to enjoy his wealth wherever he wanted. And he almost pulled it off - at one point he was up over one hundred million dollars on his trading. He could have paid back the loans and walked away with one hundred million dollars. But he was greedy. His initial success made him arrogant, and when arrogance drives trading decisions, you always lose.

Always.

Sure enough, MT began to lose money at an alarming rate and that's when Shearson decided to close his account.

It was around that time that an administrative employee of Nations Bank, unaware of the rules of contact on the Project Star loan, called Philip Morris to check on a small routine detail. The call led Philip Morris to the FBI and the FBI to Reiners. When they raided the Prudential offices that Monday morning, Reiners had lost all but thirty-two million dollars. A couple of the banks involved took suck a large loss on the loan they had to take a special charge on their quarterly earnings. They had loaned over three hundred million dollars with less scrutiny than they would employ with a car loan.

*   *   *

As the years went by and my business continued to grow at a rapid pace I was still risking most of my money everyday. The risk in options can be precipitous and sometimes difficult to measure (see mortgage derivative markets in 2008) so I was probably risking more than I had. I had recovered from the scare with the LEAPS and was very well capitalized, but my risk increased with the capital and I never anted to stare into that abyss again.

Then one day, the exchanges halted trading in Micron in the middle of the trading session.

"What the hell is going on?" I asked the exchange official.

"News pending," he replied.

My stomach fell through my feet and I could hardly draw my next breath. When the exchanges take the extraordinary step of halting a stock to disseminate news in the middle of a trading session, it means that the news is significant and will effect the price of the stock. Often times the news is a takeover bid from another company which can move a stock 25% 0r 50% or more. If Micron announced they were being taken at a significant premium, I would lose everything, and maybe more than everything,

As usual, most of the other market makers had the same risk I did and we waited for the news to be disseminated in silence. We looked at our sheets or flipped through trade tickets, not really taking in the numbers we saw. I felt like the defendant in a capital murder trial waiting for the jury to file in with the verdict.

"Micron news will be disseminated at 9:40," an exchange official announced.

Six minutes. I tried to breathe but couldn't get much air in. Six minutes. Nobody looked at me – everyone knew my risk and that it would not be a good time to approach me. I tried to not look at the clock. I perused the sheets I was holding but they looked like a bunch of random numbers. I couldn't focus on anything. I looked at the clock. Five minutes. The phone rang and I picked it up before the first ring ended.

"It's Rob," I said.

"Rob, Mark Neuberger." Mark was a trader on the desk of Morgan Stanley. Mark had sold many of the same call I had and I knew he was in the same boat I was.

"CEO resigned, our guy says it's a slight negative for the stock, maybe a percent or two."

"You sure?" I asked.

"I am," he said. I knew there was no need to ask how Morgan Stanley knew the news before it had been disseminated.

When the news was disseminated the stock was indicated to open down 1.5 percent. I would be fine, maybe even make a little money, but I still couldn't breathe and my stomach was still through my feet. The stock reopened as expected but my mind kept spinning the rest of the day without any coherent thoughts. But by the time the final bell rang, I knew that I needed to find an investor to share the risk –and the profits; I could no longer stomach the risk on my own. There is a maxim about risk tolerance: Would you rather eat well (by keeping all your profits) or sleep well (by sharing the risk)? I had plenty to eat, but wasn't sleeping well at all.

I knew there was a small pool of possible investors for a business like mine but that most, if not all, of them would make me an offer. I also knew who I would choose to be my partner.

Michael Gill was a legend on the floor. He had started in surveillance for the Exchange before going to work for a Clearing firm, then running the clearing firm, then starting an index arbitrage business and making investments in many other trading operations. He had the Midas touch and every one of his businesses was both highly profitable and well regarded. My father in law was friends with Mike and he introduced us, and Mike took the time to have me over to his office to lend me a couple hours of his invaluable wisdom. An old-school Brooklyn Irishman, Mike is a gentleman in the best sense of the word – straightforward, thoughtful, kind, loyal and honest. Even if I could get better financial terms elsewhere, I wanted Mike to be my partner.

Two days later I met with Mike in his office across the street from the exchange. I told him I thought I was ready to take on a financial partner. Before I could tell him that I would be happy to consider him if he wanted to make an investment, he started asking me questions: Why do you need a partner? What do you want the deal to protect you from? What do you think a partner can do for you? Are you sure you want to give up part of a thriving business? Will you be able to share some management decisions with someone else? It seemed as if he were trying to talk me out of the idea.

Mike took copious notes as I answered his inquiries. When he was finished questioning me, he looked up and said:

"It sounds like you have thought this through. Would you consider a proposal from Gill and Company?"

"That's why I'm here," I said.

Mike looked down at his notes again, and then said,

"I think I have enough here to draft a proposal that will address a lot of your concerns and be fair to me. Can you come back Monday so I can present an offer to you?"

The deal Mike presented to me on Monday was perfect. The terms were in range of what I knew the market for this kind of investment were and he had addressed my specific concerns in creative ways that were fair to both of us. We went over the details, agreed to a few minor changes, and shook hands on it less than an hour after we sat down. We agreed to let our lawyers draft and review the agreement and then meet for dinner to sign the final documents and celebrate our partnership.

When I arrived at the restaurant a week later, Mike was already seated at the table with three stacks of documents in front of him. We greeted each other and sat down. Mike suggested we get our business out of the way first so we could have a drink and celebrate. I agreed.

"I brought three copies of the agreement," Mike began. "One for you, one for me, and one to file with the state."

He handed me my copy and began to go through each article in the agreement so we both understood exactly what we were signing. I knew I should pay close attention but I hardly heard a word Mike said; just over his shoulder I could see a man dining alone at a table against the wall. The man looked exactly like my dad. He looked like him, moved like him, and even had a similar presence, sitting alone but not looking lonely. If I hadn't known my dad was already dead I would have sworn it was him. The more I stared at him, the more resemblance grew. As Mike talked, I watched my "dad" finish his meal, pay the server, and walk out of the restaurant. Just before he went out the door he looked over his right shoulder, made eye contact and nodded.

"Rob?" It was Mike, he had finished going through the document. "Do you have any questions?"

"No," I said, "I am looking forward to our partnership."

We signed the agreements and then had a long dinner, drinking wine and talking about everything except option trading. Mike seemed more interested in me as a person than me as a trader and partner. This continued throughout our eight-year partnership. Every time we met to discuss business, Mike would spend the first half hour asking about me, my family, and how were doing and feeling. Within a couple months of being in business together, Mike felt more like a father than a business partner, and though we are no longer in business together, he is still the closest thing to a father I have.

Wise Livelihood

"Wrong livelihood is...scheming, persuading, hinting, belittling, and pursuing gain with gain. A person knowing his income and expenses leads a balanced life, neither extravagant nor miserly, knowing that thus his income will stand in excess of his expenses, but not his expenses in excess of his income."

When I had my first success in trading and was demonstrating an ability to consistently make money in options, an old trader said:

"Welcome to trading," he told me. "You'll make a lot of money and it will buy many wonderful things. I just have one piece of advice for you: *pay cash for everything."*

He was not recommending a complete ban on borrowing. In the modern world, it is acceptable to have some debt, like a mortgage, as long as you can financially survive your own worst-case scenario. When we live within well within our means we can be happy and we do not mortgage our future for our present. It also forces us to achieve the results before reaping the rewards, which I found kept me focused and ambitious.

I consider employing somebody to be a sacred contract, almost like a marriage, where each partner has rights and responsibilities. I expected the best from my employees and in return I did *my* best to help them develop skills that would serve them in trading and in life. Being a good employer takes a lot more than paying well; it means doing everything in your power to support your employee and help them grow and improve. It was important to me that every person I hired left a better person than they arrived. I am very proud of the fact that many of the people who worked for me throughout my twenty-five year career have gone on to do great things, but I am more proud that they are all "good people."

My best friend from high school, Jon Underwood, whom I had lived with at the SAE fraternity house my first summer on the floor, had followed my career on the floor and when he graduated from UC Berkeley he asked if I could help him find a job. We were still close and loved to compete at everything – when we were at the SAE house together we would go to a dilapidated old kid's entertainment complex in Oakland where, in addition to other child-related games, they had a miniature golf course and a trampoline enclosed by a net with high ceiling. Across the middle of the trampoline was an eight-foot high net dividing it in half. Behind each side was a small opening that served as a goal in what Jon and I called "trampoline polo."

The object of the game was to bounce on the trampoline and throw the ball past your opponent into the goal. When you didn't have the ball, the trick was to time your jumps so you could block shots on goal. It sounds fun and easy but remember that the two players are bouncing on the *same* trampoline and can affect each other's jumps. Because we were both ex-football players, we had the size to really disrupt each other. This game-within-the-game became the real struggle and we awarded points for things like causing the opponent to lose balance and fall into the netting. Our games became so intense we were asked to quiet down several times.

At a kid's park.

We started going every weekend and playing for hours, sometimes into the night. We kept running statistics from our games and as in most things, were well matched. Most of the statistics were even. Toward the end of the summer we devised a World Series of trampoline polo and made plans to play it over the last two weekends of the summer. The games were to twenty-five and the idea was to play two each of the first three days with a game seven that would go to fifty, if needed, to decide it on the fourth day.

We arrived the first Saturday at noon and went into the clubhouse to rent our trampoline for the rest of the day. We were told they had changed the rules and now only rented the trampoline for an hour at a time. Being that we had never seen any other people interested in the trampolines in the many hours we had played there, we were pretty sure this new rule was aimed at us.

"Only for an hour?" I asked, anxious this could prevent the series from being played. "Can we come back then and rent it for another hour?"

"You'll have to wait for a half hour in order to let other guests have an opportunity to play," we were told and I could tell from their stiff tone that I wasn't going to be able to talk them out of this new policy. Our games lasted one and a half to two hours each so we would have to deal with a few half hour breaks but this was the World Series. When we got on the trampoline all of that vanished and we went after each other like Ali and Frazier battling for every point. Our silly world series idea had its intended effect and raised our intensity to world series level. We started quietly. The game was even for the first hour and we started to banter. As we alternated points, our volume grew. The last twenty minutes were the most competitive we had ever played, with only three goals scored, and we got louder with every rally and forgot that we had a one-hour time limit.

When I scored the last of these three goals with a spectacular lobbed shot over Jon's head as gravity drew him back down and took the first two-goal lead of the match, I let out a yawp that would have made Walt Whitman proud. It was then I noticed Jon wasn't looking *at* me, but *past* me, and I turned to see what was distracting him.

"Your hour's up," the woman from the clubhouse had her arms crossed as she glared at us.

"Oh, yeah, sorry," we replied in unison.

"Okay," she said, but she didn't move and her posture made clear she wasn't going anywhere until we were off the trampoline. After all, this woman knew how to deal with fourth- graders.

We spent a half hour drinking water and trying to stay loose but I could feel that we were being watched. It wasn't just the woman at the desk; it felt like everyone was looking at us, and not in a welcoming way. When the half hour passed we went into the clubhouse to pay for another hour but there was no one at the register. We looked around but didn't see an employee anywhere. After five minutes passed it started to dawn on me that we were never going to be allowed to play our seven-game series. I looked at Jon and without a word we walked out of the clubhouse and back to the BART station. It was not lost on us that we were kicked out of a kid's entertainment park. When we were twenty years old.

But this was the nature of our relationship and it had been hewn into us in our teenage years. When Jon decided to come to the floor, I briefly considered hiring him myself, but reflecting on our relationship, I felt it would be unwise so I introduced him to a couple of market makers I knew were looking for traders. In his first interview he was hired as a trader-trainee by two Cal graduates who were starting a market making group. Like me, Jon took to the floor like a fish takes to water and soon he was ready to trade.

Jon was very smart and, as it turns out, was a natural trader so he did well financially from the start of his career. Everything else in his life, however, fell apart. On the floor he met a great young woman and started dating her only to find out that she had a jealous and violent ex-boyfriend who also worked on the floor. The ex- started stalking them and making threats shortly after they started dating. It was a very difficult situation and went on for a year. Jon went home for Christmas after his first year of trading, borrowed his dad's car to go Christmas shopping, and forgetfully left the keys in the ignition and the doors unlocked. The car was stolen with his father's briefcase full of sensitive and irreplaceable documents in the trunk.

All of this, combined with stress of day-to-day trading, took a huge toll on Jon's health and well-being. Always an athlete and very fit, he put on thirty pounds and grew pale except for the dark circles under his eyes. Part of the struggle for Jon was a feeling that he was wasting his life chasing money every day, creating nothing and helping no one but himself. It haunted him so much that he began talking to me about leaving the trading floor. The first time he mentioned it I didn't think much of it - every trader dreams of a satisfying escape from the floor on the bad days. It wasn't until he told me had applied to the teacher training program at Waldorf schools that I realized he had been serious about leaving. Jon wanted to contribute to the world by teaching and working with kids, and that's difficult to argue with. I respected his desire to be of service and I didn't try to talk him out of it, but I did try to make sure he knew what he was doing.

Looking back now, I see we were having a conversation about *wise livelihood*.

"Look, I get it man," I said to Jon at the time. "The only thing we try to make is money and we're not helping anybody but ourselves. I don't even buy the argument that we are an instrumental piece in the capitalist economy that funds American entrepreneurs, economic growth and jobs. I'm here to make as much money as I can. That's the only goal."

"Exactly," he said.

"And living for the pure pursuit of money seemed like bullshit to me too," I continued. "But then I remembered that money is fungible and can be used for anything. Yes, it's a hollow pursuit if you hoard all your money or spoil yourself with it, but that's a choice. I've decided to embrace the greed by using my money for good."

"You're gonna go through all this hell and then give your money away?" Jon said with a laugh.

"No dude, I'm not Gandhi," I told him. "I'm squirrelling away cash to buy a house in Marin -- I'm not exactly living like a peasant. But I've found a few charities I want to help and I write them a check every time I take money out of my trading account."

"Isn't that buying your way out?" Jon asked seriously.

"Maybe," I said. "But I can tell you I volunteered at some of the same charities and they seemed to need the money a hell of a lot more than they needed volunteers."

My trading allowed me to support many great organizations including the American Diabetes Association (in honor of my Dad), The Humane Society, Save the Redwoods, Life After Innocence and The International Center for Attitudinal Healing. I am proud to know that I have been able to make meaningful donations to all of them.

Money can't solve every problem, but there are a lot of good people in the world working for excellent organizations doing great things and most of them lack the money to accomplish all of their goals. I once wrote a song with the line "you've got to have the income if you're gonna get the outcome." Sometimes, those we love would benefit profoundly from financial help due to their circumstances. It is a wise man that takes care of those he loves and a wiser one who helps those he doesn't.

Some option traders try to trade as little stock as possible because they hate paying commissions and crossing the spread rather than capturing it. They traded with more precision and are less active, willing to wait for the right positions to line up. I was not one of these traders.

I liked to trade and I loved to cobble together imprecise positions from the options order flow and manage them actively with stock. Rather than worry about paying commissions – although I did negotiate the best rates possible – I considered a big commission bill to be a sign of increased activity, which meant more opportunities. Every time I set a new personal best for a month's profit, I also paid the most commission I ever had. As the saying goes:

"You gotta be *in* it, to *win* it."

Paying one of these record bills, I joked to myself that I could hire a stock clerk to handle all my stock trades *and* a fulltime masseuse for less than what I'm paying in fees. Dismissing it as a silly thought, I paid the bills and headed to that day's Option Floor Trading Committee meeting. I arrived early and ran into Matt Adams, another market maker, in the hallway outside the conference room.

"How's it going?" Matt asked me.

"Good, but I'm recovering from paying my stock execution bill for last month," I joked. "I could have my own staff for less."

"Yeah, I had the exact same thought yesterday when I paid mine," Matt replied as we headed into the meeting.

That particular meeting was long and contentious so I soon forgot about the bill and my conversation with Matt. But on my way home, driving across the Golden Gate Bridge, I had a thought.

Perhaps it was too much risk for me to take on alone – after all, volumes can dry up like a California drought. But if Matt and I went in together, the risk was much lower.

Both of us would have to have massive slowdowns to lose money and even then, the loss would be split in half.

By the time I got home, I had decided to start an agency stock-trading desk with Matt on the options floor. After all, this was how I had started my career; SWAT Trading – which had since been bought by a bigger firm – was similar to the desk I envisioned starting with Matt. I kept trying to question the idea, but it seemed like the illusive sure thing. Even with just the business from Matt and me the firm would be profitable, and we could also attract business from other market makers. If we did, it would be a home run.

There are two risks in operating a firm like this: errors and employee embezzlement. As I've said, errors happen from time to time -- all you can do is hire good traders who have as few errors as possible.

The bigger issue is trust. Your traders are throwing around hundreds of thousands of dollars-worth of stock and may be tempted take a small slice for themselves. The oldest trick in the stock clerk book is to "sell" winning errors. Say a clerk buys three thousand shares of MSFT for seventy dollars but was only supposed to buy two thousand. If the stock is trading sixty-nine when the error is discovered, the shares are sold at seventy and both trades are added to the firm's error account, creating a one-thousand-dollar loss. If, however, the stock is trading seventy-one, the erroneous trade is a thousand-dollar winner, and there is an opportunity for a dishonest clerk to profit. An honest clerk would sell the thousand shares at seventy-one, put both trades in the firm's error account, adding a thousand-dollar profit to offset the risk of future losing errors. However, a less-than-honest clerk might have a friend who is a market maker and instead of adding the profitable trades to the firm's error account, a dishonest clerk could simply add it to his friend's account. The next day the trader might surreptitiously slip a couple of crisp hundred-dollar bills into his hand and the transaction is finished.

This wouldn't be a worry for us. Not if we hired the two best stock clerks on the floor to run our desk: my old boss from SWAT, Marc Giacamelli, and my former roommate and great friend, Peter Zavialoff. They were honest and hard-working, and they were good at what they did. Plus, they were a known commodity on the floor and as a result they would attract a lot of business. By the time I brought the idea to Matt, I had both Peter and Marc on board. When I showed Matt a business plan and a financial forecast, he said:

"It's almost too good to be true. Of course I'm in!"

We decided to name the firm Toro Trading, for the bull market, yes, but also secretly it was an acronym for *The Options Rip Offs*, the nickname stock traders called us when we bettered them on a trade.

My father's health had taken another downward turn around that time and he was no longer able to work. His medical bills were mounting. Dad was a proud man and taking money from me was killing him as surely as his health maladies. When I did help out, I would slip a check to my Mom, but Dad knew and I could feel his pain whenever we talked. I was thrilled to be able to help - to *begin* to repay him, but I understood why it hurt him so much. I told him one night during a phone call that I wanted to help more, but when I did he simply said, "no," and got off the phone.

I felt badly for pushing the topic with him but worried how he would take care of his medical needs.

Then it hit me.

Toro was the perfect solution!

Dad had recently sold his car because he couldn't drive anymore and was planning to live on the proceeds for as long as they lasted. Instead, I would have him invest it into Toro Trading, taking my fifty percent ownership share, which would entitle him to a share of Toro's profits to be paid every quarter. The money my father made from Toro supported him and Mom through the last years of his life, and the experience allowed him to feel productive. He was a proud business owner who studied every Toro statement he received and attended every meeting of the shareholders.

After Dad died, I went to help my mom sort through his things. When I opened his closet, the first thing I saw was the Toro Trading floor jacket we had presented to him, hanging by itself in the front of this closet where he would have seen it every day.

Wise Effort

"Wise Effort is more than just working hard. It is making the effort to avoid or overcome unskillful qualities, and to develop and maintain skillful qualities. Wise effort is working your best in every single moment."

.

In January 1996, eight years into my career, at the age of twenty-nine, I was elected to the Pacific Stock Exchange Board of Governors as one of three options floor representatives. The board consisted of five "floor" governors (traders from the option floor or equity floor,) seven "industry" governors (senior executives from the Wall Street firms who were our customers) and twelve "public" governors (accomplished people from outside the securities industry). I would be the youngest and least experienced member of the board and would be working with some very important and accomplished people – I served on the board with the former CFO of Kaiser Steel, the head of KPMG's West Coast office, some Silicon Valley executives, and many of the most influential players in options from the big finance firms - Morgan Stanley, Merrill Lynch, Citigroup, to name a few.

A month before my first board meeting, just before the holiday break, I spent six days and nights in a recording studio in Sausalito with my band, Low Fat Handshake, making our first album. We had been playing in clubs around the Bay Area for about a year and decided to record some of our songs while we had the chance. Back then I wore my hair long and looked more bass player than governor, but on the floor, I did dress professionally. But only out of superstition. Early in my career I wore my nicest clothes to work because I had my first meeting with my accountant and wanted to look like an adult. That day I had my best trading day ever. The next time I dressed up (for a social event after the close) I again had a record day. I spotted the trend and was quickly dressing nicely every day.

In the market, everyone is looking for correlation and often they find it where there cannot possibly be causation. For instance, the market goes up ninety percent of the years the NFC wins the Super Bowl, and down ninety percent of the years the AFC wins. Eighty percent of the time, the market is down between Rosh Hashanah and Yom Kippur. And some say the market moves up and down with the length of ladies' skirts. Perhaps my wardrobe choices were the same folly, but I got long when the NFC won, short when the AFC did, sold on Rosh Hashanah and bought on Yom Kippur so, in that context, I fully believed my clothing choice made me a better trader.

When I walked into my first board meeting, however, I could tell my suit was cheaper than all the others. I was no expert, but I easily tell the other men's suits were cut of a finer cloth and custom tailored. My suit suddenly felt like an ill-fitting burlap sack, my tie like a Jackson Pollack painting gone awry. I vowed to go to the best men's store I could find to buy a couple of tailored suits, French-cuffed shirts, and a handful of tasteful silk ties.

I quietly observed how the board went about its business and soon learned which Governors had the most influence and I studied how they conducted themselves. It was a very impressive group of people, but I had one advantage – I knew a lot more about how the floor worked than the other governors. I also sensed that the runaway success of my post, and the revenues it generated for the exchange, gave me a louder voice at the table than the other floor governors. These accomplished men and women actually wanted to hear my thoughts and ideas.

For the entire history of the Pacific Stock Exchange its biggest business was the stock trading floor. The options floor was like a little brother trying to compete for resources. Options were listed on the PSE in 1976, three years after being introduced as an exchange-traded product on the Chicago Board Options Exchange, but stocks had traded on the PSE since the early 1900s. With little respect from the staff or board, the options floor was nearly shut down a few times in its first decade.

By the time I was elected to the board, the stock floor was struggling to keep up in a rapidly changing technological environment and its market share was falling every year. The PSE was losing its niche business to new electronic exchanges like the Cincinnati Exchange because they were cheaper to operate on, losing the small share of the primary market to the bigger players whose technology could handle more volume better and faster. At the same time, the options floor was rapidly growing both in market share and overall volume, transforming itself from a slightly losing line of business to a very profitable one. The options market as a whole was growing in leaps and bounds and our share of that volume was at an all-time high so it seemed obvious to me which line of business should receive priority for resources.

When I joined the board, I learned the opposite was true: the board spent twice as much time, energy and resources trying to save the stock floor than grow the options floor. Because of its decades of dominance, there was an ingrained institutional bias to favor the stock business. I wanted to stand up and shout that this was crazy -- that any rational businessperson would focus primarily on the *growing* business rather than the withering one. And I did. Well, I didn't shout. I spoke in Board-of-Governors-speak. I knew I was the face of the options business and I felt it my responsibility to let the other governors know about our growth and potential.

When I spoke about the myriad of growth opportunities in the options market I noticed that the Public Governors were the ones listening most intently; because they were untarnished by nostalgia they had a wiser view. They were seasoned businessmen who knew how to evaluate lines of business and decide where to invest resources and they were asking a lot of questions about the options business.

The Floor Governors from the stock floor, however, did not like this and did not like me. These guys were older than me and seemed to think me an arrogant, longhaired, twenty-something prick who had no business even being on this board much less a part of resource allocation decisions. This is one reason I kept the long hair – it wasn't just for band reasons. I could tell the Stock Governors had dismissed me as an undisciplined *kid* who didn't understand how to function on a public exchange board. There is no greater advantage than being underestimated by your competition. I played the role of volatile young options upstart around them but worked hard to show the other board members that I was not only disciplined and serious, I understood the options trading business inside and out. The fact that I was competing in a top-tier name (Micron) and winning more than eighty percent of the market showed that the growth of the Exchange would come through people like me. If we could replicate my success in multiply-listed names like Micron and America Online, we could become the second largest options exchange, ahead of the AMEX, the PHLX and the New York Futures Exchange, second only to the CBOE.

During my first year on the board, the Exchange was developing a new system to revolutionize the equity business and make us competitive with the New York Stock Exchange. The revolutionary new trading system (architected by an ex-member) was called Optimark and was supposed to change the way business in the stock market was conducted.

It didn't.

In fact, when it was released, Optimark fell straight into darkness, never working properly or attracting any volume. It was shut down within a few months of its launch. With that failure, the dynamic of the board finally changed to give the options floor the appropriate amount of time and resources, which is to say almost all of them. Our average daily volume had soared from around fifty-thousand contracts per day in 1994 to over one hundred-twenty thousand and our share of the market rose from eight percent to fifteen percent. My post, which wasn't even created until 1994, was doing twenty-five thousand contracts per day.

All these facts contributed to giving me a lot of sway for a brand new (twenty-nine-year old) Floor Governor. What most of the board really wanted to know was how could we have more successes like Micron and America Online in the multiply-listed option market. The regulators were putting consistent and increasing pressure on the exchanges to list the "grandfathered" stocks of their competitors. These were the options that were listed prior to 1980 when allocations were exclusive to the exchange chosen by a lottery system. This would be a disaster for the PSE, where about sixty percent of the options volume traded in these exclusive listings. Another twenty-five percent traded in two multiply listed stocks, Micron and America Online, both of which were allocated to me.

The Outside Governors wanted to know how I had gotten the market share in two of the most active option stocks of the time.

"We don't do anything that other specialists don't do," I explained. "We just do it consistently, in every situation. That means, every customer who comes into our market, no matter the market conditions or the size of the order, receives the same impeccable service. We know that one bad customer experience can destroy months of excellent service so we never let down our guard or let our financial performance or risk affect the customers' experience. The Pacific is a small exchange. It's cheaper and easier for firms to route their order flow to a larger exchange so we need to do things the larger exchanges don't. We give the best experience to every single customer, every single time."

This was met with a moment of silence. I realized they were looking for a method or some special sauce that could be replicated. Finally, one of the senior Public Governors spoke,

"Soooo," she drew out the one syllable word so it sounded condescending. "You try harder?"

"No….," I said slowly, looking straight at her. "I try better."

*   *   *

At my first meeting, the board formed committees to address various areas. I was only interested in one - the Exchange Technology Committee - and was able to get on it. As it is for most businesses, technology investment and development were the most important decisions to be made, and I wanted to be a part of them. Especially at that time, technology was the new storefront: "location, location, location" used to drive real estate decisions but now "technology, technology, technology" was our mantra. On the committee I pushed the exchange to devote more time, money, and resources to the options trading systems. Revenues had exploded on the options side of the business and I argued for all of this money to be invested in our systems. By the end of my first year, the exchange had doubled its options technology budget and was hiring developers as quickly as possible.

But not fast enough.

Volume surged again and the already overloaded exchange systems could not keep up; more volume means more data and our system could not process it in real time, which meant the market data the floor traders depend on, was stale. This is (obviously) not acceptable; we were pricing options based on where the stock *used* to be. It is impossible, or should I say unprofitable, to make markets in options without knowing the *current price* of the underlying stock. It didn't take long to see that the data the Exchange was providing was latent and even when your markets are wrong, plenty of customers will come to you. Likewise, if we halted trading, our customers would route their orders to another floor and may not ever come back. We needed to find another way to know what the current market was. We had a computer linked directly to the NYSE but it didn't give quotes on stocks, it was only an interface to enter orders and receive fills. I was discussing the reality of halting trading with an exchange official when my stock clerk interrupted me.

"Why don't I just buy and sell one hundred shares over and over," he said. "We will see a price every ten seconds or so and not lose very much money."

"Brilliant!" I replied.

We used this technique to get through many difficult times and I used the anecdote to effectively urge the board to spend more money addressing the issue. Some days we even ended up profitable on all the one hundred share orders we executed.

*   *   *

Much has been written about the value of hard work: "the early bird gets the worm," "nothing worth having comes easy," "the only place success comes before work is in the dictionary," the list goes on. And these are, for the most part, truisms. We must always strive to do the best we can in everything we do. And doing your best usually means hard work and hard work makes the outcome more satisfying. But *wise effort* is more than working long hours at the office, taking extra reps after practice, or answering emails on weekends. In fact, the most important work we do is working hard to be present and aware in each moment, at work and away from work, with everyone you see.

Distractions are born in moments where we stop working to be present and aware. Whether you're having a conversation with your spouse or an exchange with a salesman, if you are not present you will miss part of what you hear and often that will ultimately become a distraction. In any career if you use *wise technique* in your approach you will be more efficient, able to work longer, and achieve better results. Wise effort is smart effort. It is diligence in *every* moment to be your best. It is bringing the same effort to everything you do professionally and personally. It is being a good professional; but it's also a good friend, colleague, spouse, parent, sibling, son/daughter. Many people work so hard in one area of their life (like their job), they are unable to bring wise effort to the rest of their lives. This is just as dangerous as not working hard at your job.

I began my meditation practice without knowing that I was doing it. I have always been the kind of person who likes to stare out a window, daydreaming. Without fail, nature stills my mind so I often take walks or hikes when I need to think. Most of my best trading ideas came to me during those solitary times.

When I began to study Buddhism, I realized that all of that was a form of meditation. Rather than having to concentrate on meditating, clearing my head came naturally to me. I love to think about nothing and I'm always curious about where my thoughts lead. Buddha taught about many differ types of meditation including walking in nature; you don't have to be cross-legged on a cushion in a temple with incense burning to be meditating.

I found that an hour of meditation was almost always more profitable than an hour spent staring at stock charts and options prices.

*   *   *

On October 17, 1989, I was walking through the parking lot of Candlestick Park for game three of the World Series when I suddenly came to a halt. Oakland faced San Francisco in game three of what was nicknamed 'the Bay Bridge Series' and my friends and I were thrilled to be there but on our way into the Park I felt a strange vertigo. As I wondered what was happening, car alarms started sounding all over the parking lot, and someone yelled:

"Earthquake!"

The next tremor, an aftershock, arrived like a wave rolling through the ocean, only instead of the ocean, this was a parking lot full of cars. It was over as quickly as it had begun. A cheer went up around the stadium, there didn't seem to be any damage and an earthquake seemed appropriate for the Bay Bridge Series. I was, in fact, still able to sell my extra ticket to that night's game to another fan as I resumed walking to the stadium.

Once there, I noticed that the giant escalators that carried fans to the upper decks, were not operating. I looked around -- all the lights were out as well. Still not concerned, I climbed one of the escalators to my seat in the first deck. When I arrived, it was apparent that the people on the deck had a different experience of the earthquake than I did. Looking down the aisle, I noticed small pieces of concrete debris all over the steps and realized these were little pieces *of the stadium.* Then I noticed a woman in the front row was hysterically sobbing and holding on to her seat like it was still moving while her friends tried to talk her into getting up and leaving the stadium. I heard later that the decks of Candlestick Park were *designed to bounce* in an earthquake, breaking its cement façade but staying structurally sound. That woman in the front row had evidently had quite a ride.

Down on the field, the players, coaches, and umpires were milling around second base – as far away from any part of the structure as they could get. Knowing the game wasn't going to start anytime soon I walked back down the escalator to the esplanade. On the way I saw a group of people crouched around a portable TV set and just as I wondered what they were watching and if they might have an update on the game, one of them stood up and yelled:

"The Bay Bridge is down!"

Oh, shit.

This was more serious than I thought. As more information about the damage caused by the Loma Prieta earthquake filtered in, it became clear there was not going to be a baseball game. I walked back to my car hoping to meet my roommate there and drive home. We had a "secret" parking spot we liked about a half mile from the stadium right under the freeway; we were young enough to trot the half mile and beat the traffic lined up to get out of the stadium's massive parking lots. On my walk to the car I saw some damaged buildings - broken windows and fallen facades – and for the first time wondered if my building was damaged.

My roommate, Pete, was waiting for me at the car, listening to a transistor radio.

"The Bay Bridge is down?" I asked.

"Yeah," he said. "And the Embarcadero Freeway and the Nimitz. Most of the freeways are at a complete standstill, traffic's not moving at all. And I just heard the Marina is on fire."

The last part was particularly worrying because we lived in the Marina.

"What are we going to do?" I asked him.

"We're gonna go home," Pete said as if he hadn't just told me the freeways were impassable. "I'll bet I can get us there in half an hour."

This would be indeed impressive -- it took twenty minutes on a regular day, but Pete grew up in the city and knew the San Francisco streets well.

Twenty–eight minutes later, we crested the hill in Pacific Heights and started down to the Marina. We could see smoke everywhere but it was hard to tell where it originated. Unsure how bad it would be around our building, we parked the car a few blocks away on Green Street and walked down to our apartment on Greenwich Street. Our building appeared undamaged so we went inside. The elevators weren't working so we took the stairs up to our apartment. No damage, not even a broken plate. I could hear voices on the communal roof deck of the building so we climbed the stairs to see what was going on.

The roof door was propped open with somebody's ice chest. Several barbecues were already fired up and the deck was littered with ice chests filled with food and drink.

"Hey!" a guy who lived on the second floor greeted us. We'd never met or even spoken with him but he was greeting us like a long lost relative.

"Power's off so empty your fridge and freezer and join the feast," he said. "You can cook on any grill that has space."

We met everyone in the building that night, most of them for the first time, despite having already lived there a year. The rooftop party went on late into the evening, but I snuck out early to go to bed because the market was going to open at 6:30 the next morning whether San Francisco was ready for it or not.

I woke up in darkness at my usual hour. Our power was still out and I was pretty sure it would be out downtown, too, but I cleaned up, shook off my hangover, and drove to the exchange. As soon as I got near the building, I saw traders milling around on the streets outside the exchange. I found Barbara Newton and asked her what was going on.

"The building might not be safe," she said. "The Fire Department is going in now to assess it."

I joined some other traders on the street to wait for news. The market would soon be open and we needed to access out positions and trade. When we were told that the exchange did not expect to open again for at least a few days, there was a collective cry that sounded like a provoked mob. We needed to attend to our positions anytime the market was open or risk losses. It was expiration week and there was a lot of trading to do before our October option expired on Friday. The head of the exchange told us to make sure our clearing firms knew where to reach us and they would come up with a plan.

That afternoon I got a call from an exchange official. He told me that all the market makers were invited to trade their stocks on another floor. The Chicago Board Options Exchange (CBOE), the American Stock Exchange (AMEX), the New York Stock Exchange Option Floor (NYSE options) and the Philadelphia Exchange (PHLX) would each recreate a number of our pits. The exchange chartered a plane from Oakland, the closest operational airport, to drop off traders in Chicago for the CBOE and then New York for AMEX and NYSE and PHLX. The traders going to Philadelphia would get there via helicopter from New York.

I would be going to New York to trade on the AMEX. The exchange told me that the AMEX required members to wear a suit and when I looked in my closet for the one suit I owned I remembered it was being cleaned. I ran to the dry cleaner, but it was near the fire site in the Marina and was chained up, closed. Back home, I started calling department stores hoping to find one open. I finally reached someone at Nordstrom on the outskirts of San Francisco, in the Stonestown Galleria. They were open for a few more hours, he told me. I drove over with Pete who was tired of sitting in the dark apartment. Just inside the main doors of Nordstrom, in the store's café, there was a TV tuned to news. Pete looked saw it and told me he'd wait for me there and walked over to join a small crowd watching the worst images of the earthquake. Video of the Marina on fire, the Bay Bridge section that fell, and the collapsed East Bay freeway were looped on the screen.

"Can I help you?" asked a well-dressed but unshaven salesman.

"I need a suit and I need to walk out of here with it in an hour," I said.

"You came on the right day," he replied, thankfully non-plussed.

Twenty minutes later I was in the café watching the news with Pete while my new suit was being tailored. I saw that the Bay Area Rapid Transit (BART) was restoring service and the first train to go through the tunnel under the Bay to Oakland would leave San Francisco at five o'clock. I knew I would have to be on it. A half an hour later I had my fitted suit and we left for home.

I packed quickly and Pete gave me a ride to the Embarcadero BART station. When the Oakland-bound train arrived, I piled in along with the rest of the passengers. There were about ten people on the train already, but instead of being spread around the train car like commuters usually are, they were sitting close together. I joined them. The train began descending into the trans-bay tube, and we all sat quietly looking out the windows. I saw water drip on the train window and began to panic. I learned later that it is normal for there to be moisture in the tunnel, but at the time I feared it was the dam breaking.

We made it through the tube and back up from underwater and I relaxed as I settled in for the twenty-minute ride to Oakland airport. When I finally walked into the terminal, I heard a familiar hum and sure enough, I saw traders all over the place, but mostly in the bar. Exchange officials were huddled at one of the airline counters. I went to join my colleagues at the bar.

It was a very raucous scene. Traders were drinking fast and sharing their earthquake stories for the first time. Stories they are still telling today. We stayed in the bar as long as we could until finally it was time to go through security and board our flight. There was almost nobody else in the terminal so we were on the plane in no time. It was a charter so as soon as we were on board, the plane took off. Flying over the San Francisco Bay we could see the entire city, but from our height it looked as beautiful and inviting as ever. Once we were in the air, the plane began to resemble the terminal bar. It certainly had the same buzz. Somewhere over Iowa, we finished the last of the alcohol (or so they told us) and most of us tried to get some sleep. We landed in Chicago and the traders destined for the CBOE deplaned. When we took off for Newark I fell asleep for the first time.

We hit the ground running in Newark.

A fleet of limousines was waiting for us on the tarmac and we were whisked off to the AMEX. You can never say New Yorkers don't treat guests well, even their competitors. When we arrived at the AMEX building in the heart of Wall Street AMEX staff led us to a bank of elevators and up to the members' dining room where a breakfast buffet awaited us: bagels and lox, platters heaped with pastries, eggs benedict and mounds of bacon and sausage.

I had barely eaten in the last twenty-four hours and was battling a hangover so I filled my plate generously with a little of everything. While we were eating, the opening bell was nearing. It was eight-thirty in the morning in New York, the market would be open in an hour. When we all finished breakfast, we were led to conference rooms to change clothes, and then were ushered to a briefing room where we met the staff. The AMEX officials explained where we would trade and the rules we would follow. With the opening bell about to sound, I stopped listening and started thinking about my portfolio.

I walked onto the floor of the American Stock Exchange for the first time and the only thing I wanted to see was a quote machine to find out where Microsoft was trading. I had a huge October position and could do well if it continued its recent rally so I found a quote machine, typed in MSFT and then hit 'enter.'

Microsoft was up a whopping six dollars!

I almost shouted for joy. If I could sell stock at that current price I would make three times more than I ever had in a single day. I looked around and saw stock clerks but knew they would never take an order from someone they didn't know. I asked around and evidently the other PSE traders were having the same problem. I was long more than twenty-five thousand Microsoft and needed to lock in my profit. I called Steve Vogel at MASH, a guy I knew from my SWAT days.

"Hey man," I said, relieved he picked up right away. "I gotta sell ten thousand Microsoft anywhere."

"Where the hell are you?" he asked.

I explained the situation and asked if he would trade with me.

"You have to come through a broker or I can't get it into our system," he said.

"I'll sell it a quarter under the bid," I said, desperate to lock in my profit.

"Dude, you could offer it a buck below," he replied. "I can't do it."

I hung up the phone in a panic. I was living a recurring nightmare I used to have wherein I have made a lot of money but have no way to secure it, to lock it in.

I saw one of the AMEX officials who had briefed us earlier in the day behind a nearby post talking to the specialist. I pushed through the large crowd (there to trade Apple) and made my way behind the post, a place I had been specifically told we were never allowed.

"Hey, you can't be up here," an exchange guy blocked my path. Before he could continue, though, I frantically explained the situation.

He seemed impatient and didn't seem to be listening to what I was saying. Then I heard a voice behind me.

"You just need to sell stock?"

It was the specialist the impatient exchange guy had been talking to.

"Yes!" I answered as I turned to him.

"You know how to work an Instinet terminal?" he asked.

"I do," I told him. "I started as a stock clerk."

"Well, just go ahead and sell it here on my terminal," the benevolent stranger said. "We'll figure out the clearing later."

I couldn't believe how easily he offered to solve my problem. A prayer had been answered.

I quickly punched up Microsoft. The quote loaded slowly and I waited. Then I saw it. The stock was now up NINE points. I sold thirty thousand shares of Microsoft as quickly as I could. With the stock up an additional three points I was even longer but I decided to let the rest ride.

"How's it going?" the specialist asked later on.

"All done for now," I replied. "I can't thank you enough."

"Andy Schwartz, AGS Specialist," he said, extending his hand to shake.

"Rob Kovell," I shook his hand. "I'm an independent on the P-coast."

"I hope all your family and friends are safe after the earthquake," Andy said.

"They are, thanks," I said. "You know, it's really not as bad as the news makes it seem. All they show are the few small pockets of destruction. Most of us weren't affected beyond losing our power."

"Good to hear. Come back in an hour and I will have found a way to get your trades into your account," he said, turning back to his specialist duties.

Andy was taking risk for me -- if the stock kept rising and I (a trader he didn't know) denied making the trades he would be responsible for the loss. Andy helped without worrying about his risk, and all he cared to ask me was if my family was okay after the earthquake. When I think of all of the soulless people I met in this industry, I think of Andy, too, and I feel better.

Wise Mindfulness

"May we exist like a lotus,
At home in the muddy water.
Thus we bow to life how it is."
-Zen Proverb

Throughout my career, I traded the most volatile stocks in the one of most volatile markets of all time. Technology in the nineties and two-thousands evolved so rapidly that some companies couldn't keep up. America Online was one of the hottest stocks in the world in 1995, just as Blackberry-maker Rhythm in Motion was in 2005. Motorola and Nokia were the dominant players in mobile phones until Apple changed everything with the iPhone in 2007. Microsoft and Intel were still growth stocks, but not the tech behemoths they are today.

I traded Microsoft through the first six years it was public, AOL through its rags-to-riches-to-rags race, and Micron when memory prices were swinging wildly. Any day a bad decision or unexpected event could have bankrupted me. On the floor this is called *blowing out.* Blow outs are spoken about in hushed tones like a death. Anytime there was a large move in a stock, the crowd would count heads to make sure everyone survived. I once saw a strangely structured takeover of a company called Vista Chemical blow out an entire crowd, requiring the exchange to issue a rare "call for capital" which requires members to report to that pit and make markets.

Whether it was an unpopular, lousy trader or a major competitor, no one takes pleasure in a blow out and almost always takes a second to mourn the occasion.

Sometimes a trader would just disappear, never to be heard from again, leaving the crowd to wonder how he "blew." Because these were the stakes, confrontation was a big part of the floor culture, and in markets like these, with the extraordinary volatility and risk and opportunity, it sometimes got out of hand. The alley behind the exchange floor building, which led from Pine Street to the underground parking garage, was where the physical confrontations took place (until the Floor Trading Committee ruled it had discretion to suspend members for actions not just on the floor but anywhere near it).

The pressure affected different people in different ways. Some were able to handle it, others were not. There was no single way to deal with the pressure; those who were able to handle it, did but those who didn't often chose alcohol or drugs and ultimately never lasted long. The techniques for coping run the gamut: from silence to singing or yelling, stillness to arm waving fury, mocking others or yourself. I was a singer. I would get a song in my head, usually related to the market action: Tom Petty's *Freefallin'* or REM's *End of the World As We Know It* in a down market, and Cracker's *I'm a Little Rocket Ship* or David Bowie's *Space Oddity* during violent rallies.

There was a young trader from Indiana named Terry who started in our pit fresh out of college. He was the embodiment of *aw shucks*: polite, straight in every sense, small town Midwestern boy. After his first day, the betting started on how long he would last and the over under was set at two months. The first time the pressure got to Terry, as it does everybody, he looked down, shook his head and said,

"Gosh darn it!"

The crowd, accustomed to hearing a minimum of two forms of the F-word in every curse, paused for a second to make sure he wasn't being ironic, then erupted in laughter.

When Terry looked around bewildered by the laughter it spurred more hilarity. When the laughter settled down and the betting began, the over/under fell to three weeks.

Throughout his first week, Terry continued to use words that sounded as foreign to our ears as our curses did to most people – "shoot," "dang," and "poop" were among his favorites. It sounded like second grade recess to us, and everybody who bet the under started counting their money. The next week, just as we were getting accustomed to his non-vulgar vulgarities, Terry missed a trade that he needed to hedge his account.

"God *damn* it!" he said.

No laughter this time.

There was a suspiring sense of disappointment; we had all secretly hoped he could survive uncorrupted in our environment. But after his increased profanity, Terry stood up straighter and looked more relaxed. A few moments later, his stock clerk reported to him that he had missed the trade again.

"Shitfuck," he said under his breath as if to see what would happen.

The line on the over/under shot up to six months.

This process continued for weeks then months until Terry became the biggest curser in the crowd, then on the floor, and then the most profane person I had ever known. He surpassed the creative swearers from my football locker room days and all my years on the floor. Terry's combinations of swear words, animals, and himself sometimes made *me* blush. It somehow worked for Terry though, and the over was the right bet; he went on to have a long successful career on the floor, cursing the whole way.

I am not recommending high level swearing as a good way to handle pressure, although admittedly a good loud "FUCK ME!" did relieve a little pressure once in a while. But I learned it was a temporary relief, the affects gone before I could really feel them.

Micron became the busiest stock option in the markets in 1995 and the pressure over the next few years was as intense as it was incessant. Sometimes I handled it well. Other times, I did not. I had my fair share of irrational, emotional outbursts and sometimes took my frustrations out on others. As I said, confrontations are a regular part of interacting on the trading floor, and often the strength of someone's aggression is much greater than the offending transgression that provoked it. We called this the *Next Guy Rule*.

Stress would build up in a trader over a series of perceived slights from brokers, a bad break in the market, a stock clerk missing a trade, until someone would say something to that trader that would normally be a minor annoyance that provoked little if any response. However, with the trader already at the boiling point, this person gets the full explosion of the trader's pent up frustration directed at them. It is not because of what they said, but that they were the *next guy* to say something. When I did this, I would often apologize later to the recipient by saying, "Sorry, next guy rule."

In the late nineties, when I was in my early thirties, I noticed that the emotional toll of trading was affecting me more than it ever had. I was unable to sleep for more than four or five hours a night, I always felt tired and alternated between eating too much and being unable to eat. I starting going through a roll of antacids every few days and felt like a stereotype. I tried to relax but every week seemed to bring a volatile or stressful event or five.

Then one day, a large and complex order in Micron options came into the crowd. It required us to sell stock at a certain price to offset the risk of the options we would trade. I offered stock at the appropriate level. As specialist, I am generally entitled to half the order, so I offered enough stock to trade half the contracts. After I gave my stock clerk the order, a retail broker with a small problem that needed special attention distracted me for a few seconds. When I turned back, my stock clerk told me I had sold all of the stock I had offered. I turned to the broker with the large order.

"Done your way," I said. "I'll do half."

As I started writing up a trade ticket, the broker looked at me.

"Traded ahead," he said. "I'm out."

I felt a red cloud fill my mind and body. He was telling me that another trader had already traded the order -- while I was dealing with the customer service issue.

I had missed it.

Now I would need to buy the stock back at a loss. All fair by the written exchange rules, but if you want to get along in a specialist crowd you need to give certain courtesies to the specialist. If you don't, he won't give any to you, and you will struggle in his crowd. One of these courtesies is telling the specialist when you are about to trade an entire order that he is offering stock against. I just stared at the broker.

"Who?" I asked.

He turned and collected the trade tickets from a young trader I barely knew who stood in the back and usually traded very small. He worked for a very good trader named Trent Cutler, and was clearly acting on Cutler's behalf. I knew Trent well and we shared a mutual respect, so I could have called him and almost certainly worked out an amicable resolution.

But I didn't.

Instead I exploded on the young trader who, though he should have known better, looked confused, like he didn't know what he had done wrong. I unleashed a prolonged tirade: yelling, gesticulating, insulting, and threatening. I got so angry I felt the coffee in my stomach rage like the Atlantic Ocean in a hurricane. I could see the young trader wither under my stream of words until he looked half his original size. I stopped abruptly, turned away, and walked as fast as I could to the exchange floor bathroom, crashed into a stall, threw up my breakfast and continued retching far past the point where I had emptied my stomach.

When I finished I flushed the toilet and stood up in the stall I felt dizzy and weak, my head throbbed and my hands were still trembling from my tirade. I could barely walk off the floor and take the elevator up to my office where I collapsed on the uncomfortable couch. Lying there, I slowly came back into myself. The shaking stopped. My stomach settled and I began to get my strength back. I decided that I could not put myself through this kind of emotion any more, the physical toll was too obvious to ignore. I was in my thirties, already old for a floor trader, and knew I needed to manage the pressure better or I wouldn't survive it much longer. There were plenty of examples of traders who lost their nerve (and with it their money), as they got older; there was a certain look and movement to their eyes, as if they had seen too much to believe anything. I knew I never wanted to be one of them.

In order to avoid that fate, I knew that I had to prevent my emotions from getting the best of me as they had that day. The physical cost was high but there was a financial one as well. My anger had prevented me from acting wisely and calling Trent Cutler to work out a solution. I was not yet a self-identifying Buddhist – I thought Zen was a complete lack of emotion. Lying on my office couch, recovering from my outburst, I decided I would become the "Zen Trader" and trade without the emotions that were causing me so much stress and costing me money. I had been trading almost a decade and had been through just about everything -- I certainly didn't need to react to every little thing. Or to anything. I would be (what I thought was) totally Zen in the pit: unflappable and emotionless. I was too old for this shit!

I found it very easy to be at peace in the pit, and for a week I was as unflappable as the guards at Buckingham Palace. I reacted to nothing and felt no emotion. I was a machine, responding to input rationally and quietly. Only problem: I lost money every day. Not a lot, but definitely steadily red every day. On a bike ride that weekend I thought about how poorly I had traded that week and wondered if I could be a Zen Trader *and* make money. The results from the week suggested the fire of my emotions was the edge between profit and loss.

Later that weekend I drove out to Muir Woods and went for a long hike. There, among the ancient trees, I came to understand that my emotions were like racehorses pulling me in a wagon: without constant attention (mindfulness) these horses would run wild and drag my wagon until its wheels fell off and it broke apart. Even then, wild horses will not stop running, they'll drag you around in the dirt without the wagon. If you simply cut yourself free from the reins you will stop being dragged through the mud, but you will also watch the awesome power of a team of wild horses run away over the horizon.

I had cut loose from the reins believing this made me a *Zen Trader,* but without my team of racehorses to propel me I was no match for the market. On my hike in the woods, I decided to end the Zen Trader experiment and allowed myself emotions. Anger, frustration, sadness, outrage, pride, spite, confidence, courage, elation – I considered each one, I could feel their strength and was elated to have them back.

The market wasn't very different the following week but I made money every day. I was mindful of my emotions and when I felt one rising, I took care to examine its effect on me and then I'd harness its power into my service. I found I could hold my anger steady and use it to focus my mind rather than let it distract me. I learned how to show flashes of it to the other traders when it served me in the fray of trading, but not let it get away from me. I reined in my pride so it gave me confidence and courage rather than temerity and folly. I enjoyed every good trade without becoming over-confident and careless and felt frustration when things went poorly without allowing it to change the way I trade.

Wise Concentration

"You should sit in meditation for twenty minutes a day unless you are too busy. Then you should sit for an hour."

Meditation was the most powerful trading tool I ever experienced. I meditated often and in many different ways and I discovered it is the path to prosperity and joy. If you feel silly trying, stop judging. Meditation is really just deep thought without the convention of prejudice and judgment. There is no way to say it otherwise; my success in finance was a result of daily meditation. It made me a much better trader. And person.

*   *   *

"Do you know Irv Kessler?" asked Barbara Newton, on a rare visit to my office.

She had knocked on my door as soon as I came back to my office after the market closed. An unexpected visit from my risk manager would have been alarming if I had been having any struggles with my trading; a visit from Barbara usually meant d the clearing firm wanted you to put up more money. But it was January and we were coming off of our best year and having an even better month and our trading capital was at its highest point. Things were going so well that that very weekend I was taking my firm on a ski trip on the slopes of Squaw Valley near Lake Tahoe.

"I've heard of Irv Kessler," I said to Barbara. "He runs that big Chicago operation that just got bought by Knight Trading, right?"

Knight was a publicly listed company that specialized in electronic stock trading. They had bought Irv's Chicago-based company as an entrée into options trading.

"That's him," Barbara said. "He asked me if he could call you. Evidently he has some questions about trading out here on the Pacific."

It wasn't the first time a trader from another exchange wanted to ask me about the Pacific. Our tech-focused listing strategy had paid off and we were the fastest growing exchange in the country. No trader wants to miss a good run.

"Sure," I said. "Any day after the close."

"Well, if you can do it right now, he's available," she said. "I can call him from your phone and introduce you and then let you talk."

The urgency was a little strange, but traders are an impatient lot and I was free so I agreed and handed her my phone. She dialed the number from memory and told someone she had me on the line for Irv Kessler.

"Hi Irv," Barbara said into the phone. "I've got Rob Kovell here for you. Yes, you're welcome. Anytime."

She handed me the phone and left the office.

"Hi Rob, Irv Kessler," a Midwestern-accented, cheerful voice said.

"Hi Irv," I replied. "What can I do for you?"

"As you may know my company was recently bought by Knight Trading," Irv said. "They...uhh... *we* are looking to deploy more capital on trading floors, specifically in specialist posts," Irv said.

"The Pacific is our first priority," he added.

I had led the formation of lead market maker posts on the Pacific; I ran the largest post, and I'd been vice chairman of the exchange so it wasn't unusual that Irv would seek my advice before establishing a post for Knight. Though they would be competition for valuable new allocations, their presence would bolster the exchange and attract new business so I was pleased to hear they were coming.

"Though I'm not on the board anymore and can't speak officially for the exchange," I said, "I can tell you they will be thrilled to have Knight in the LMM program. You'll have to apply for LMM status, but once you're approved the exchange will create a post for you rapidly."

"Yes, well, we have already gone through the process and are approved as an LMM," he said.

"That's great!" I said, "I'd be happy to do anything I can to help you out here. It does take some time to build a post."

"Well, that's the thing," Irv replied. "I've learned a few things in my short time here at Knight. The first is that when they do something, they do it big. We want to establish a large, multi-floor market making business."

"I see," I said, though I didn't.

"Which brings me to the reason for calling today," he continued. "Knight is interested in purchasing your post, the Micron Post in San Francisco, and we would…"

Finally understanding the purpose of the call, I interrupted him.

"Well, thank you for the call, but I'm not interested in selling," I said. "We've got a great staff and the post is booming. This company is my life, I couldn't sell it."

"Alright, you sound certain," he said. "We're going to be looking at other posts in the coming months but if you change your mind please let me know. Thanks for your time."

I had received inquiries before, the most serious from Apollo Trading, the company of CNBC personalities Pete and Jon Najarian, but trading companies weren't valued with the same metrics as other businesses due to the volatility of our earnings so offers were low by standard measures, the range was usually two to three times earnings. The S&P usually trades between fifteen and twenty times earnings and technology stocks are purchased for thousands of times earnings.

On the drive home, it occurred to me that I had violated the trader's code of always listening to buyers. After all, everything is for sale at some price -- and I hadn't even asked what they might pay!

That led me to wonder why was I so attached to owning the post? What if they were willing to offer me a huge amount of money? I definitely had my stresses running the firm; it had grown to nearly fifty employees in two locations, San Francisco and Chicago. I often complained that I spent so much time running the business that it cut into my trading.

It was early 2000 and our tech stock dominated post was rocking; the NASDAQ was on its historic rise to five thousand, which it reached in May (and then not again for fifteen years) before starting its equally historic fall. In the five years since I started the LMM post, our earnings had grown significantly. Everything pointed to that continuing. Of course Knight wanted our post now: we were perfectly positioned and growing.

That Friday, when we left for the Squaw Valley trip, our capital was once again at a new high. So was my self-esteem. My assistant, Gail, had planned the trip and arranged for me to get VIP treatment so when I arrived at the resort I was treated like a king. Though being fussed over usually made me uneasy, I enjoyed it completely on that trip. At dinner that night with most of my company, I watched as they shared stories (often about me) and laughed with each other. They were a great group of hard-working, quick-witted, honest young people and I swelled with pride to see them gathered in their civilian clothes. When I stood up to toast them and our success, I felt weightless.

It was the Martin Luther King holiday weekend and I was thrilled to have three days of skiing. The snow was great and the weather forecast positive – sunny and crisp both Saturday and Sunday with a small storm expected Monday night. *Perfect*, I thought. We would get in two and a half days of skiing and still beat the storm back down the mountain. We met early the next morning at the resort chairlift and took it to the top, gathered, and then pushed off together, heading down the mountain like Custer's cavalry attacking at Little Big Horn. The best skiers were quickly out in front racing back and forth across the slope and doing tricks where they could; the rest were making more conservative turns on the groomed run, weaving around each other. Recent bonuses had been good, so everyone was feeling joy as we stormed down the mountain, hooting and hollering at the top of our lungs.

Over the next few runs we divided naturally into smaller groups effortlessly formed according to a complex formula of rank, seniority, age and ability. I skied with the five other traders who worked in the Micron post with me every day; luckily, we were all good skiers and the conditions were perfect, but my favorite part of the day was riding chairlifts and chatting with my colleagues about all the things that never come up on the trading floor.

Sunday was much the same except that our joint run was at the end of the day because people had straggled onto the mountain at various times depending on their participation in the previous night's activities. That night we had rented a room at the finest lakefront restaurant in Tahoe City and, although we were all exhausted from trying to out-ski each other, the room was filled with energy and laughter, which barely dimmed even during the meal. I again looked around the room at my staff and felt a swell of pride - this is what had become of my decision to drop out of UC Davis to try my luck on a trading floor.

I woke up Monday morning and my room was still pretty dark so I lay in bed and looked forward to our final day of skiing. We had agreed to meet early and ski hard until two in the afternoon so we could get off the mountain ahead of the storm. As I lay there in bliss, the phone rang.

"Hey Rob, it's Scott."

I looked at the clock. It was only 6:45am.

"Hey man, what's up?" I asked, "you ready to ski?"

"Have you looked out your window?" asked Scott.

I rolled out of bed, opened the curtains, and saw a scene that looked like the inside of a snow globe just shaken.

"I guess the storm got here early," I said.

Normally this would be heaven - a day of powder skiing is a rare blessing - but we had to get our staff back down the mountain that day or we would face catastrophe when the markets opened. We had left a skeleton staff behind but they would only be able to manage our positions. They would not be able to service all the customers in our pit and one bad day of service can cost you months of business. Relying on the skeleton staff was a worst-case scenario.

"We gotta get the hell out of here," I said, finally realizing the stakes.

"Yup," said Scott. "I already called Gayle and she is calling all the rooms. We have to wake people up and tell them to be in the lobby ready for departure by 7:15am. The front desk said the pass could close by nine."

We were on the road within a half an hour but Donner Pass was a mess because the California Highway Patrol (CHP) was allowing only ten cars through at a time. The trip over the pass usually takes less than an hour, but that harrowing day it took us almost five with winds gusting in every direction, blankets of snow falling, visibility poor, and cars sliding out. I'd driven over the Donner Summit hundreds of times and this was the worst weather I had ever seen. My knuckles were sore from tightly gripping the steering wheel.

We made it out of the mountains around noon but still had a three-hour drive across the valley ahead of us. Trying to get my carful of employees home to recover from the weekend, I pushed my speed well over the limit and just as we got to Sacramento was pulled over and ticketed for speeding.

By the time I dropped off my passengers and got home it was five o'clock, nine hours after our hurried departure. My neck was so stiff and painful I took some Advil and went to bed. Exhausted, I fell to sleep immediately, but then woke up shortly after midnight with my neck and back in deep spasms that were overwhelmingly painful. I slid out of bed and onto the floor where the pain was almost bearable if I stayed in a certain position and didn't breathe too deeply.

In the morning, I went to the doctor and was told I had bulging discs in my neck. The only treatment was ice and rest, followed by physical therapy. For two weeks I was unable to do much besides sit in a chair and ice my neck; I even slept sitting up in the chair because lying down was excruciating. When I started physical therapy, I soon learned it, too, would be uncomfortable. I was manipulated in painful ways and had to do exercises that hurt even more. It was almost a month before I could return full time to trading and even then, I was in a lot of pain.

Our results had slumped during my time away and competition was increasing; and not from other small fish like me but from huge fish like banks and hedge funds that had not previously thought our pond was big enough. My market share was eroding and my competitors were getting stronger.

At the end of May, the LMM post had not quite broken even for the year. Expenses were higher and the competition was shrinking our already narrow margins. As I reviewed our financial data for this period there was nothing positive about it and comparing it to previous years made it look even worse. Our market share was at its lowest point in several years and continued to steadily, if slowly, decline. I decided to spend every trading day in June in the pit trading - something I had not been able to do consistently for more than just the last few months. The neck injury had exacerbated the problem, but already my time was increasingly taken up running the business, which prevented me from being in the pit where I could add the most value.

Or do the most damage. Which, in the end, is what I did.

June is a slow time on the market so there are always plenty of sellers in the June options. Knowing this, we lowered the prices far enough that we thought even with less activity in the market we could be profitable. But it seemed like every one of my most important customers wanted to sell the June options and we ended up long more than we would have otherwise. One week into June we were three times longer on some June options than we wanted to be.

And that is when the music stopped.

Or, more accurately, that's when Micron's movement stopped.

We lost a few hundred thousand dollars in the following two weeks until finally the June options expired. The worst kind of loss, a slow drip everyday building until, after a couple weeks, the worst outcome possible arrives. It's the opposite of quickly tearing off the bandage; it's more like Chinese water torture.

I left the floor after the close on expiration Friday feeling as low as I ever had walking off that floor. I knew I needed to be outside, so I went straight home, changed clothes, loaded my mountain bike onto my car, and headed for my favorite trail up Mt. Tam.

Railroad Grade is a long and gradual climb up the mountain that traces the route the railcars used to bring tourists to the top when Marin was mostly filled with summer homes for wealthy San Franciscans. It was my favorite climb because of the steady effort it required: a climb not so hard that I had to focus on pushing, but hard enough to occupy my body and free my mind, allowing me to get deep into a meditation. As I rode up the mountain, the racing thoughts bouncing around in my head began to slow down so I could see them as a whole, rather than one crisis at a time.

In a single instant, about ninety minutes into my two-hour climb, I decided I needed to sell the post.

All arguments pointed to selling except for one. My ego. But on the mountain meditating that day that ego fell away as instantly as it had risen. I got off my bike when I reached the summit, stretched my body, and breathed. My breath came easier and deeper than it had in a long time. There was not a single doubt anywhere in my mind that I would do what I had five months earlier rejected out of hand: I would sell my business.

First thing Monday morning, I began to do exactly that.

My first call was to Irv Kessler at Knight and within minutes I was negotiating with his head of trading, Peter Harris. The June debacle left us down a significant percentage for the year, making it difficult to argue about a multiple of our earnings, and I worried that risk would scare them away. This, I thought, would be the trickiest part of the negotiation.

But when we got on the call for the first negotiation, Mr. Harris began,

"We've done a few post acquisitions already and have developed a method for valuation," he said. "I have to warn you that one thing we do not want to see is your profit and loss. We don't care what you were able to make in the post because we think we have a good way of measuring how we will do and that is the only thing relevant to us. I hope you weren't hoping for a large multiple on your earnings because we won't even ask what they are."

"Well, that's too bad," I lied. "But I understand."

It wasn't *too bad*, it was *perfect*. I couldn't understand how they thought they could model earnings without past data being relevant but hey, Harris sounded pretty sure of himself.

"We will run our model based on the exchange data," he said. "We can get you a number tomorrow."

That first number was twice what I was hoping to get. I could barely breathe when I heard it. One of my closest friends, an investment banker named Peter Holbrook, had advised me that no matter what they bid for my post, I was to say the following three sentences:

"Thank you for the interest. I have to think about it and discuss it with my people. I'll get back to you tomorrow."

Which is exactly what I said.

It was a good thing I had sought Holbrook's advice, otherwise I may have shouted "SOLD!" like the floor trader that I was. Instead, I drove straight to Peter's office, filled him in and asked him what to do.

"Remember," he began, "they are a giant corporation. They're used to doing things analytically and slowly, working to a price through a series of negotiations. If you accept the first bid it will scare them and they may do more due diligence. You don't want that."

"No-I-do-not," I said emphatically, thinking about my loss for the year. "What should I do?"

"Counter them fifty percent higher," Holbrook said. "And plan to meet them in the middle."

There is a fallacy that all traders are good negotiators. Although some traders are also good negotiators, many are not. A trade and a negotiation are as dissimilar as a back-of-the-napkin sketch and a Picasso painting – they require very different skills. I could sketch anything quickly and move on to the next, but I could never spend weeks creating a masterpiece.

Peter sensed my reticence and made me promise I would do what he advised.

After sleeping on it, I woke up determined to follow Peter's wise advice.

The market opened unchanged and volume was light to non-existent; it was slow summer Thursday with more people heading out of town than to their broker's office. My call with Peter Harris wasn't until one-thirty, a half an hour after the market close. I looked up from my post after the opening and saw it was only seven-fifteen. My heart sank; I knew it was going to be the longest trading day of my career.

I was right: it was.

When the closing bell rang I went straight to my office, locked the door, turned out the lights and waited for the call, silently rehearsing what I was going to say. The call came and I launched right into it.

"Thank you all so much for the interest in my post and for making an offer for it," I said. "I want to see the post continue to thrive under the expertise and capital you can provide, but my analysis tells me the post is worth more than you offered. I think X-million would be a more appropriate valuation."

There was a long silence during which my heart did not beat. The other feelers I had put out with prospective buyers had led nowhere. If I lost this deal I would get nothing but the regret of passing on double what I originally wanted to get. I'd end up with nothing.

Finally, Harris broke the silence.

"Well, we'll have to sharpen our pencils, take a closer look, and see if we can get there," he said. "We'll try to get back to you tomorrow, but more likely it will be early next week."

Although this was what I expected, I could feel my breathing shorten and my heart rate accelerate. I knew two things: It is normal for a deal this size to take time, number one and the second thing I knew was that I was going to be a wreck until they called back.

Friday went by with no call.

Again, what I expected. But again, disappointing. The weekend felt like it lasted a week but finally it was Monday.

I prepared myself for the call to come in the afternoon, which is when traders usually turn to non-trading-related business. I had managed to have decent day trading so I went up to my office and turned the lights out to wait for the call. As soon as I sat down at my desk, my phone rang. I took three deep breaths and let it ring twice more.

"Rob Kovell," I answered.

"Hey, it's Jamie."

My floor broker was calling, which usually meant he had an error he needed help with.

"I just saw someone come to the office and ask for Mark Volpe and Pete Martinez," he said.

Mark and Pete ran the second largest post on the PSE and had a firm similar to mine.

"The guy said his name was Steve Harris," Jamie said. "Weren't you talking to Scott about him?"

Evidently, Jamie overheard me telling my head trader to come get me if Peter Harris called.

"*Steve* Harris or *Peter* Harris?" I asked.

"Steve," he said. "I heard him say it twice."

"Okay, thanks man," I said. "That's good to know."

"Anything going on I should know about?" Jamie asked.

Yes, I thought to myself, *you should know I am negotiating to sell the post where you work. You may be working for Knight in a month instead of Kovell Trading.*

"No," I told Jamie in as calm a voice as I could muster. "I just need to keep tabs on that guy. Let me know if you hear anything else."

I hung up the phone in a panic.

Knight was talking to the next biggest post on the PSE. Mark and Pete might hit their first bid leaving me out in the cold. I had heard Peter Harris had a brother working for him and apparently that brother was now out to lunch with my competitors. I wanted to call Peter Harris and yell into the phone, "Sold! Done your way!" but this wasn't a trading crowd. The rules of engagement were different. This was a negotiation and until the deal was signed and approved, nobody would be held to anything. If they bought Mark and Pete's post, there would be no bid for mine.

Although I no longer expected them to call, I stayed late in my office just in case. I told myself that up until a bike ride a week ago, I had never wanted to sell so if the deal never happened I should be happy to continue running the post. Six months ago, I wouldn't even listen to what Irv Kessler would offer me for the post, so why was I now so attached to this deal? I realized that I had allowed myself to think about the sale and the proceeds I would receive, and in doing so, I had become attached to the outcome. There was no going back. I needed to sell the post right away.

I went for a strenuous hike up King Mountain in Larkspur trying to work the angst out of my body and mind. I meditated, breathed, and prayed. Although my body was tired when I got home, there was little sleep for me that night. I went to the office the next day knowing I'd have to trade an entire session before I might hope to hear anything.

I tried to focus on my trading, which I usually couldn't crowd out of my mind, but now felt irrelevant. Going through opening rotation I couldn't remember what month of options were trading or how I wanted to price them. I let Scott take over and went to the back of the crowd. I looked across the floor to Mark and Pete's pit and saw Mark standing in the back of the crowd with a man that had to be Peter Harris's brother, the fraternal resemblance was clear.

"Breathe," I said to myself.

I stood in the back of my post pretending to study the screens on the side of my pit while I looked past them to study Steve Harris and Mark Volpe. I watched as Pete Martinez joined them and soon all three left the trading floor together. I stood there blankly looking at the trading screens while hurricane force winds swirled the thoughts in my brain. I would not be able to focus on anything until I heard again from Peter Harris. I wanted to go up to my office and sit in the dark and pray, but I knew I needed to be on the floor all day so everything would appear normal. It was the longest trading day of my career and by the end of it I was certain I had lost the deal.

I went straight to my office and sat down at my desk. I sat there for a minute in the quiet office before deciding to take off my trading coat to settle in for what I feared would be a long wait. Just as I was taking off my coat, before I could even free an arm from it, the phone rang.

I pulled the coat back on and answered the phone standing next to my desk chair.

"Rob Kovell," I said into the phone.

"Rob, it's Peter Harris," I could tell he was on speakerphone. "I'm here with my team. Did we catch you at a convenient time?"

"Absolutely," I said, wondering if there were anything in the world that could make this call inconvenient. "What can I do for you?"

He started in a disappointed tone of voice and my heart sunk. He talked about the competitiveness of the business, the higher expense of doing business on the Pacific, and he also mentioned he had been speaking to some of my competitors. I prepared for him to say they were rescinding their offer and buying someone else. Then, his tone brightened.

"We are looking to get exposure to tech volume and your post has some exciting allocations for us," Harris continued. "Unfortunately, we can't get the valuation high enough to justify paying your offer."

An interminable pause.

"But we could meet you half way," he said.

Exactly what Peter Holbrook had told me would happen a week ago on our first call! It had sounded so simple then but had been interminably complex actually going through it.

"Peter," I took a deep breath and exhaled relief and joy. "You've just bought yourself a trading post."

The end